DIALOGUE
WITH

ERIK
ERIKSON

DIALOGUE
WITH

ERIK
ERIKSON

**WITH
REACTIONS FROM
ERNEST JONES**

Richard I.
Evans

JASON ARONSON INC.
Northvale, New Jersey
London

THE MASTER WORK SERIES

First softcover edition 1995

Copyright © 1964, 1967, 1981 by Richard I. Evans

Library of Congress Cataloging-in-Publication Data

Evans, Richard I. (Richard Isadore), 1922–
    Dialogue with Erik Erikson / by Richard I. Evans.
      p. cm.
    Originally published: New York : Praeger Publishers, 1964.
    Includes bibliographical references and index.
    ISBN 1-56821-561-4 (softcover : alk. paper)
    1. Erikson, Erik H. (Erik Homburger), 1902–
  2. Psychoanalysis. I. Title.
  BF109.E7E9 1995
  150.19′5′092 – dc20   95-14657

Manufactured in the United States of America. Jason Aronson Inc. offers books and cassettes. For information and catalog write to Jason Aronson Inc., 230 Livingston Street, Northvale, New Jersey 07647.

To my lovely wife and children

Foreword

Since the publication of the first edition of this book, the wisdom of Erik Erikson's focus on psycho-social development through all the stages of life-span development into maturity is even more pronounced. For example, the special problems of aging and of identity—particularly as highlighted by the leaders of the woman's movement—are provided as a useful theoretical framework by Erikson's ideas presented in this volume. The continuing concern with problems of youth, becomes particularly meaningful in terms of Erikson's conception of the "identity crisis."

Most importantly, Erik Erikson has posited a model of human development that has become increasingly important to behavioral and social scientists in exploring almost every issue in contemporary society, even among those who are less psychodynamically oriented than he is. His approach to psychohistory is becoming of interest to many disciplines outside of the behavioral and social sciences.

The lucidity of Erikson's ideas as presented in the first edition of this volume led to substantial interest in it. This new edition will provide an opportunity for an additional readership to share many of Erikson's major ideas through a spontaneous dialogue.

As a fascinating study in contrast, this volume includes a somewhat briefer dialogue with the British psychiatrist Ernest Jones. In Paris, at an International Psychoanalysis Meeting in August 1957, just prior to his death, I was fortunate to complete these dialogues with Dr. Jones, Freud's loyal supporter, friend, and biographer. A penetrating thinker in his own right—as reflected, for example, in his intriguing analyses of Shakespeare's works—Jones remained to the end a biologically oriented, orthodox psychoanalyst who, in the absence of Sigmund Freud himself, can be regarded as a formidable spokesperson for Freud.

Professor Erikson departs from Freud's focus on a biologically deterministic, psycho-*sexual* analysis of human development. Erikson focuses more on social and cultural determinants of behavior with his psycho-*social* model of human development.

Unlike many of the so-called neo-Freudians, such as Karen Horney and Abram Kardiner, who became in many respects cultural determinists, Erikson maintains a finely tuned balance between the importance of the orthodox psychoanalytic view of psycho-sexual development and his particular integration of cultural and social influences in his stages of psycho-social development. As can be perceived in the dialogue with Dr. Jones—who unflinchingly states that man is after all an animal whose behavior must be examined in terms of more biologically programmed impulses—his view leaves very little room even for the more modest culturally deterministic view of Erikson. Yet interestingly enough, with the advent of the socio-biologists and their insistence on the importance of genetic programming in human behavior, Jones' views at times seem more viable today than they might have in 1957 when we completed this dialogue.

I am pleased to reprint this dialogue, which was originally unobtrusively presented as part of an earlier volume, *Conversations with Carl Jung.*

Acknowledgments

In the long process involved in filming and taping the dialogues with Erik H. Erikson and transcribing, editing, and integrating them into the present volume, I am indebted to a great many individuals. Though space prohibits mentioning everyone who so kindly assisted in this venture, I wish to express my appreciation to at least some of these individuals.

The skill and imagination of psychology graduate students Judith Woodard and Martha Frede are significantly reflected in this volume, and for their efforts during the early stages of preparation of this volume I am most grateful.

Thanks are also due to psychology graduate student Peter Leppmann for his assistance in the final editing of the manuscript which in particular included the integration of Erikson's reactions to the first draft, and the important details connected with developing and checking out the bibliography.

Grateful acknowledgment is made to the University of Houston for permission to utilize the printed texts of the filmed and taped dialogue. Mr. James Bauer of the University of Houston, who functioned in the demanding role of technical director for the taping and filming sessions, should also be mentioned among those who have greatly assisted me.

At several points in the project we were fortunate to have the services of some able secretaries. In this respect I wish to express my thanks to Mmes. Ellen Roberson and Carolyn Ramirez for their preliminary work on the manuscript and to Mrs. Peggy Leppmann, who with great patience and care handled the demanding chore of preparing the final form of the manuscript.

I am grateful for the support from the National Science Foundation, without which this project could not have been implemented.

Finally, the wonderful cooperation of Professor Erik H. Erikson cannot be emphasized enough. Not only was he willing to participate in the filming and taping sessions which are involved in this project, but in spite of his extremely busy schedule, he was willing to edit and even in some instances amend the text of the material in printed form, so that this volume would not suffer in the transition from film and sound to print.

Contents

Contents

Preface

The dialogue contained in this volume, as has been the case in the two previous volumes in this series, provides a vehicle through which it is possible to sample many of the major conceptualizations of one of the world's notable contributors to personality theory. In this volume a reflection of the significant contributions of Professor Erik H. Erikson, which he has presented through his many books and articles, is presented here within a single framework. This volume, then, is potentially valuable to the reader who is relatively unacquainted with Erikson's work, providing, as it does, a relatively comprehensive and lucid overview of his psychology and general philosophy of man.

To the reader who has previously read a considerable amount of Erikson's work, this material should also be of interest. One can observe how Professor Erikson feels *today* about many of the ideas presented in his earlier works. Furthermore, certain new ideas and areas of focus are suggested. In addition to communicating the content of Erikson's ideas, it is hoped that the dialogue reveals a feeling for his gentle, thoughtful personality—more clearly in this context than in his more didactic writings.

This volume is the third in the series, which is based on edited transcripts of the 16-mm. sound films and additional audio-taped dialogues with such notable contributors to personality psychology as Erich Fromm, Gordon Allport, B. F. Skinner, Henry Murray, Gardner Murphy, and Raymond Cattell. *Conversations with Carl Jung and Reactions from Ernest Jones* [16] and *Dialogue with Erich Fromm* [17] were the preceding volumes in this series. Also in this series presently is a dialogue with playwright Arthur Miller, which represents an experiment in attempting to allow the psychology student to sample the thoughts on personality psychology of a great contributor to the humanities.

RICHARD I. EVANS
Professor of Psychology
University of Houston

Introduction:
Perspective on an Innovative
Teaching Device

The present volume constitutes the third in a series based on extemporaneous dialogues with some of the world's outstanding contributors to the understanding of personality. Designed as a teaching device, the series was launched in 1957 with completion of such dialogues with the late Carl Jung and Ernest Jones supported by a grant from the Fund for the Advancement of Education, and is being continued under a current grant from the National Science Foundation. A basic purpose of the project is to produce for teaching purposes a series of films recording these dialogues which introduce the viewer to our distinguished interviewees' major contributions to the fund of personality psychology. It is our hope that these films will also serve as historical documents of increasing value as significant contributions to the history of the behavioral sciences.°

The volumes in this series are based on edited transcripts of the dialogues which include the text of additional audio-taped discussions as well as the content of the films. It is our hope that these dialogues in the print medium will extend the primary goals of the films: (1) to introduce the reader to the contributor's major ideas and points of view; and (2) to convey through the extemporaneous dialogue style a feeling for the personality of the contributor.

Since the structure of this volume reflects an innovative approach to teaching, some of our concerns regarding the proper communication of its intent might be shared with the reader. When we completed the Jung and Jones book [16], we thought the word "conversation" could best be used in the title to describe its process and content. However, we soon discovered that this seemed to imply to some potential readers of the book something a bit more casual and superficial than we had intended. As indicated

---

° The films are distributed by Association Instructional Films, 600 Madison Avenue, New York, N.Y. 10022.

earlier, an attempt is made to emphasize spontaneity in our interaction with our participants; this we feel adds a dimension to the project that is not usually present in more didactic forms of teaching. Yet, although these encounters are extemporaneous, we are hopeful that this does not detract from any significance that the content may have. We would hope that a relatively informal discussion with an outstanding contributor to a discipline, as he seriously examines his own work, will not be of less significance by virtue of its informality.

A more detailed description of the philosophy and techniques of this project is reported elsewhere [16]. However, a few points bearing on the content of these volumes might be emphasized here. First of all, since the questions are intended to reflect most of the published writings of the interviewee, it might be expected that a comprehensive summary of his work is evoked. However, because of the selectivity necessary in developing the questions so that the discussion can be completed within a limited time interval, it would not be fair to say the results of these sessions—either in the films, which reflect the content emanating from only about half the time spent with the participant, or even in the books, which reflect about twice the amount of time—necessarily provide the basis for an adequate summary of the contributor's work.

Perhaps more than a comprehensive summary, we are hoping to present a model of a teaching technique which may become an additional means of compensating for the trend observed among many of our students today to become increasingly content with secondary sources to gain information concerning our major contributors in the various disciplines. The material resulting from our dialogues provides a novel "original source" exposure to the ideas of leading contributors to a discipline. Hopefully, this in turn may stimulate the reader to go back to the original writings of the interviewee which develop more fully the ideas presented through our dialogue. In fact, the term "dialogue" was finally adopted instead of "conversation" to describe our content and method to imply merely that it represents a programmed teaching effort, in the more traditional Socratic sense. However, the interpretation of the term "dialogue" within the current academic scene often also implies a "challenge" to the individual being "interviewed." Furthermore, to some the term "dialogue" suggests that the questioner is simply using the individual being questioned as a tool to project his own (the questioner's) teaching role into this situation. My own goals here would preclude either of these interpretations of the term "dialogue." It is my intention that these dialogues reflect an effort to produce a constructive, novel method of teaching, and cast my interviewer role neither as the center of focus nor as "critical challenger." I would feel that the purpose of this project has been realized if I am perceived as having merely provided a medium through which our distinguished interviewees can express their views. It might be mentioned that our interviewees are so generously willing to contribute their time to these efforts in the spirit of the teaching aims of this project. This became evident, for example, in a letter from the late Carl Jung, reproduced in the first chapter of *Conversations with Carl Jung and Reactions from Ernest Jones* [16]. Furthermore, using such sessions as a background for critical examination of the views of the participants, might better be left to another type of project, since even if this "critical set" were to be included in my questioning, it might be difficult both to introduce the reader to the contributors' views and to criticize them as well, within our limited time commitment. In fact, I would expect that some of the individuals who agreed to participate in our project would not have done so if they had sensed that this would become the context for a critical attack on their work.

In the last chapter of this volume, I have attempted to state some current trends in personality theory which became the background against which I formulated the questions used with each of the participants in this project. Without anticipating the details of this discussion at this time, it seems nevertheless appropriate to call the reader's attention to one thread which runs through the questions which were developed, namely the use of Freudian theory as a base line for them. As a result of my experience in teaching personality theory over the years, I have found that emphasizing the ways in which various theorists agree or differ with traditional Freudian theory becomes a valuable tool for teaching. Of course, the relevance of such an orientation is more apparent in the case of individuals such as Jung and Fromm (the subjects of the first two books in this series), and certainly this is so in the case of Erikson, the subject of our present book. Of course, it would be much less applicable to, say, the subjects of our projected later volumes in this series, such as B. F. Skinner and Gordon Allport.

Now to the organization of the book. The present volume is organized in accordance with certain divisions of subject matter which I planned as I programmed the questions. In the first section my questions are designed to develop a discussion of Erikson's eight stages of man. Of particular interest to the reader here is a discussion of Erikson's significant conception of the "identity crisis," looked at not only from the standpoint of the developing adolescent, but in the broader sense as it is relevant to other problems in a culture.

The next section, which deals with his cross-cultural and psycho-historical studies, provides for Erikson an opportunity to discuss these unique investigations and analyses, which not only provided some of the bases for formulating his eight stages of man, but illustrate some of the intriguing insights resulting from Erikson's examination of broader human problems.

In the next section, Erikson reflects on his relationship with psychoanalysis, indicating where he agrees with, disagrees with, or expands Freud's psychological and philosophical concepts. Here he also has an opportunity to discuss his views of some of the techniques of psychotherapy, and critically evaluate psychotherapy in a broad as well as a technique-oriented sense.

As indicated earlier, the final chapter is an expression of some of my own views, including an introduction to approaches to personality psychology stemming from the theoretical trends of biological, cultural, and self-determinism, and Erikson's position with respect to these trends, which may help the reader to place the dialogue in perspective.

Particular attention is called to the references to Erikson's published works in various footnotes throughout the book. The author has selected references which bear special relevance to specific areas of the content of the present volume. The excerpts to which the reader is referred not only allow him to observe ways in which Erikson in the dialogue may have altered or extended ideas and concepts presented at an earlier date, but also present in many instances a more elaborate discussion of topics not discussed in great detail in the dialogue. The author hoped in this manner to add to this volume a facet which may enhance its value as a teaching device, particularly for the reader who is relatively unfamiliar with Erikson's work.

In the case of Carl Jung, the subject of the first volume in this series, utilization of the dialogue technique hopefully facilitated a degree of clarity of expression which frequently is not evident in Jung's own writings. In the case of Erich Fromm and Erik Erikson this rationale would, of course, not apply. Fromm, the subject of the second volume in this series, demonstrates great clarity and skill in communication in his own published works. Erikson, too, represents in his published works an effective skill in communication. But it is hoped that one unique service provided by the dialogue presentation in the case of writers like Fromm and Erikson is to allow the reader either to be introduced to or to re-examine some of their ideas through a relatively extemporaneous situation, as they are coalesced from the particular point of view inherent in the questions which guide the discussion.

It should be pointed out, however, that in his writing, as Erikson expresses himself in his own unique style, he has the opportunity to rewrite and to polish until he deems the finished product satisfactory. In the spontaneity of our discussion, however, he is called upon to develop his ideas extemporaneously. We hope that this element of spontaneity may assist in penetrating to the "man behind the book" while losing none of the ideas central to Erikson's thought. Because preservation of this naturalness of communication is essential to the purposes of each volume in this series, few liberties have been taken with the basic content of Erikson's responses to my questions, although some editorial license had to be exercised to shift effectively from oral to printed communication, in the service of readability. In fact, Erikson was given the opportunity to later edit and expand answers to some of my questions, in the service of doing justice to some of his responses which—because of time limitations—appeared incomplete in our first transcription of the discussion sessions.

So this dialogue as it is presented here duplicates insofar as possible the tenor of the exchange between Professor Erikson and myself as it actually took place. In spite of some of the editing which was necessary in both Erikson's responses, as indicated above, and my questions, it was a pleasant surprise to review our hours of discussion content and see how few deletions and alterations were required. We hope that the flow of material, though extemporaneous, is sufficiently well organized to make this a worthwhile teaching tool. Also we hope this makes available to the reader some reactions not readily obtainable from Erikson's traditional didactic presentations.

When confronted with a man like Erik Erikson, who so graciously consented to participate in our project, one is tempted to try to gain some notion of what he is like as a human being. It would be presumptuous, of course, to imply that I could evaluate definitively a man of his complexity on the basis of a few hours of interaction. However, to those who know him he is a remarkable man. His quiet, tolerant, analytical style belies his incisive perceptiveness. A little of his background and present activities may also be of interest to the reader. Erikson entered psychoanalytic training from the field of art. As an artist, he obviously brought an unusual perspective to psychoanalysis. Through his training with Anna Freud he became one of a group of pioneer child analysts. From his earlier life in a diversified European culture, he came to the United States. Here he developed a distinguished career as a practicing psychoanalyst, cross-cultural investigator, author, trainer of psychoanalysts, and professor at Harvard University. In fact, he is considered by many as one of the most exciting and popular instructors currently on the faculty of Harvard. From this versatile background, he emerges as a most unique and creative individual, whose works are commanding an increasing amount of serious attention.

In conclusion, I would like to reiterate that in the dialogue which follows, the questions presented to Professor Erikson are designed to allow his views to emerge as coherently yet as spontaneously as possible. If the balance between immediacy and consistency becomes upset occasionally, I trust that the reader will forgive me; in the context of such extemporaneous discussion it is difficult enough to maintain a logical progression without the added distraction of cameras, recorders, film and sound crew members, and others whose presence was necessary during my exchanges with Professor Erikson. In fairness to him, I must point out that this was a situation far from ideal for him to be expected to produce a polished presentation of his ideas. However, under the circumstances, I feel that our objective of an integrated presentation, maintaining the atmosphere of essentially free exchange, was adequately realized. With this view I hope the reader will agree.

1. The Eight Stages of Man

¶ DR. EVANS: Professor Erikson, to begin our dialogue it might be interesting to explore your provocative analysis of the eight stages of man.° Although these formulations admittedly have their roots in Freud's work, you have added various innovative dimensions. For example, as we all know, Freud presented a very important model of psychosexual development. He felt that during the first five years of life, in the biological unfolding of the indi-

° For a systematic discussion of Erikson's developmental stages see *Childhood and Society* (New York: W. W. Norton, 1950, 1963), pp. 247–74. This section of one of Erikson's major works presents an excellent background against which to consider much of the discussion of this chapter.

vidual, he was confronted with a series of conflicts which he resolved with varying degrees of success. Through what he called a repetition compulsion, reflections of these early patterns of the first five years continue to be operative later in life. We thus would understand a good deal of man's later life as a reflection of his successive conflict resolutions in his early life. Freud did not emphasize to the same extent development in periods after these first five years. It seems that you not only try to conceptualize these later periods in more detail, but have developed an analysis of man's over-all development in these eight stages of man. Perhaps we could discuss them stage by stage and view them, where applicable, relative to Freud's psychosexual developmental sequence.

Oral-Sensory Stage: Trust vs. Mistrust / Hope

The very first stage Freud talked about was a narcissistic or self-love level of development, which included a preoccupation with the oral zone. You also speak of an oral-sensory level. Throughout your eight stages, you have some character dimension in a psychosocial development parallel to Freud's psychosexual development. At this first stage, you talk about basic trust versus basic mistrust being related to this oral-sensory level. Now could you tell us a little bit about what you mean by basic trust versus basic mistrust as it evolves from this oral-sensory level?

PROFESSOR ERIKSON: I see, Dr. Evans, that you want to develop this dialogue rather systematically and with an emphasis on differences. If so, you must permit me a few remarks first. When I started to write extensively about twenty-five years ago, I really thought I was merely providing new illustrations for what I had learned from Sigmund and Anna Freud. I realized only gradually that any original observation already implies a change in theory. An observer of a different generation, in a different scientific climate, cannot avoid developing a field if it is a vital one. Even a great breakthrough like Freud's is characterized by a passionate concern to bring order into data which "haunted him," to use Darwin's phrase, for very complex reasons of his own and of his time. One can follow such a man only by doing likewise, and if one does so, one differs. I say this because some workers want to improve on Freud, as if his theories were opinions, and because they prefer nicer or nobler ones. But the scientific climate has changed so much that older and newer theories cannot really be compared. One knows only that without the older ones, newer ones could not have emerged. Freud's original formulations were based on the imagery of a transformation of energy.

¶ This would reflect the effects of nineteenth-century physics.

꘎ That's right. Today we are guided by concepts such as relativity and complementarity, even where we don't know it. So Freud's attention to the origins and the transformation of sexual energy was not an expression of a pansexual philosophy. Sexuality seemed to him to be the most likely area in which quantities of excitation could be found which rise out of body chemistry. And here, the theoretical configuration fits both the data and the job, because there was something almost palpably quantitative that had become excessive or repressed or both in the patients of his time. But only the stubbornness and the courage in the face of his own inner conflict and of universal rejection made possible Freud's great finding that sexuality does not begin in puberty but develops in distinct stages. He became aware of the possibility that the "oral stage," for example, contributes instinctual energy to normal sexual activities as well as to perverted ones, and to neurotic inhibitions as well as to character formation. He realized that psychopathology could make a fundamental contribution to "normal psychology." But normality and pathology change with cultures and each period contributes new insights. So we are interested here in what orality may contribute to the child's psychosocial development, and now I am ready to answer you. Orality —that is, a complex of experiences centered in the mouth —develops in relations with the mother who feeds, who reassures, who cuddles, and keeps warm; and that is why I refer to this first stage as the oral-sensory and kinesthetic one. The basic modality of behavior, at this stage, is the incorporative mode. The first thing we learn in life is to take in. We take in not only with the mouth, but also with the senses, and you can see the child trying even with his eyes to "incorporate" and then to remember and then to recognize outside what is, as it were, already in him. Now, the basic psychosocial attitude to be learned at this stage is that you can trust the world in the form of your mother, that she will come back and feed you, that she will feed you the right thing in the right quantity at the right time, and that when you're uncomfortable she will come and make you comfortable, and so on. That there is some correspondence between your needs and your world, this is what I mean by basic trust. You see, in animals this is all given in the instinctive equipment. In man it must be learned, and the mother is the one who must teach it. Moreover, mothers in different cultures and classes and races must teach this trusting in different ways, so it will fit their cultural version of the universe. But to learn to mistrust is just as important. That is why I speak of basic trust and basic mistrust. And, if you don't mind my registering a gripe, when these stages are quoted, people often take away mistrust and doubt and shame and all of these not so nice, "negative" things and try to make an Eriksonian achievement scale out of it all, according to which in the first stage trust is "achieved." Actually, a certain ratio of trust and mistrust in our basic social attitude is the critical factor. When we enter a situation, we must be able to differentiate how much we can trust and how much we must mistrust, and I use mistrust in the sense of a readiness for danger and an anticipation of discomfort. This, too, is certainly a part of the animal's instinctive equipment. We must learn it in terms of our cultural universe.

¶ In a sense, then, you are filling in a gap in Freud's work by adding the dimension of psychosocial development, which Freud didn't really develop very far. Perhaps he might have if he had continued working.

Yes, but I must repeat that we can now recognize, for example, in his early dream reports that in a sense he knew all this, but he had to establish one thing at a time, and his great contribution was psychosexuality. It is a mark of a great man that he watches jealously over the expansion of his field. He makes sure that certain principles do not get lost before they can be superseded.

¶ Now, to get back to this matter of basic trust and mistrust, it's interesting that such aspects of psychosocial development are at the basis of some of the fundamental virtues which you schematized in your contribution to a volume by Julian Huxley on *The Humanist Frame* [9] and have elaborated in your last book [12]. You seem to tie in the virtue of hope with this first oral-sensory level.

Yes, this is true. For Darwin's one-hundredth birthday, Huxley edited this book on certain humanist interpretations of evolution, and he asked me (he can be an inspiring editor) whether there was something I might have wanted to say for a long time that would fit into such a plan. As I anticipated, there was no chapter on childhood in his plan! It seems almost impossible to believe, at least for a psychoanalyst, that the plan of a book like this should not include a systematic discussion of the long childhood that has evolved for man, together with a specialized brain, cultural institutions, and so on. So I tried to formulate for this occasion what I thought were the basic human strengths. Somewhat challengingly, I called them basic "virtues," in order to point to an evolutionary basis of man's lofty moralisms. You see, hope is a very basic human strength without which we couldn't stay alive, and not something invented by theologians or philosophers. You may remember Spitz's studies° in which he shows that children who give up hope because they do not get enough loving and not enough stimulation may literally die. Now, if the word virtue causes a bit of discomfort to a lot of people, I hope it will eventually make a point. Religions only sanctify what they recognize as given if they concern themselves with hope as a basic human attitude which must be transmitted from parent to child and be restored by prayer. By this I do not mean to imply that the highest Hope is "only" a facsimile of the earliest, but that the whole plan of man's concerns develops in ontogenetic stages. And in this context, hope is the basic ingredient of all strength. In Old English the word "virtue" could be used to describe the strength of a medicine, and you could say that if it had stood around too long it had lost its "virtue." So this is what I mean by it—something vital, that animates, and is "the soul" of

° The observations referred to here are reported in detail by R. A. Spitz in Ruth Eissler, *et al.*, *The Psychoanalytic Study of the Child* (New York: International Universities Press), Vol. 1, 1945, pp. 53–74; Vol. 2, pp. 113–7 and 313–42.

something. Animals, again, are born with something akin to hope. But in man, because of his lifelong struggles between trust and mistrust in changing states and conditions, it has to be developed firmly, and then be confirmed and reaffirmed throughout life.

Muscular-Anal Stage: Autonomy vs. Shame and doubt / Will Power

¶ The first stage then for man would be the development of hope emanating from a favorable ratio of trust versus mistrust. As you have referred to the second stage of development, we see the emergence of the muscular-anal stage, which is likewise related to the Freudian narcissistic level of development. I think those who are familiar with the Freudian theory of character have always thought of fixation at the anal level as leading to various character traits relating to saving, hoarding, and so on. But you are not really referring to a character trait that develops from a fixation. Rather you are referring to a psychosocial trait which will develop in parallel terms with this anal level; you have described these traits as autonomy versus shame and doubt.

That's right. We have to consider that the anal musculature is part of musculature in general, so that the child entering this phase of his development must learn not only to manage his sphincters, but his muscles and what he can "will" with them. Now the urinary and anal organs are, of course, tied in physiologically with psychosexual development, and also with aggression. Just think of swear words! It would, of course, only be in cultures in which cleanliness and punctuality are overemphasized for technological and sanitary reasons that the problem of anal control might develop into a major issue in childhood. But the shift from the first to the second stage also marks one of those difficult human "crises." For just when a child has learned to trust his mother and to trust the world, he must become self-willed and must take chances with his trust in order to see what he, as a trustworthy individual, can will. He pits his will against the will of others—even that of his protectors. Cultures have different ways of cultivating or breaking this will. Some use shame, which can be a terrible form of self-estrangement for the human. On the other hand, one cannot imagine a human who is not afraid of being embarrassed—afraid of being in a situation in which other people will find him shameful. This is the age when the child begins to blush, which is a symptom of knowing one is being watched (from the inside, too) and is found wanting.

¶ So, autonomy will result from constructive resolutions of feelings of shame and doubt that develop during this muscular-anal level?

👣 Yes. Again, a ratio is necessary to development here.

¶ I think we should underline the point you made earlier. In considering this polarity, you're not saying that ideally one quality should be produced and the other not at all. Both must emerge out of this developmental stage.

🦷 Yes, but the ratio, of course, should be in favor of autonomy. If in some respects you have relatively more shame than autonomy, then you feel or act inferior all your life—or consistently counteract that feeling.

¶ It would probably be unheard of that a person would develop without any shame or doubt.

🦷 Yes, because all of this is intrinsically related to evolution. Man is the animal that stands up and is naked and for whom the face and the eyes become so very important for social perception. Shame, for example, in Eastern civilizations, is expressed in terms of "losing face," a most terrible experience.

¶ In terms of the virtues you have been describing, another parallel from the scheme you introduced in Julian Huxley's book [28], as we discussed earlier, is the development of will power. Now that seems to logically follow, doesn't it, from what you said?

🦷 It does to me.

¶ I think you almost anticipated this when you talked about how the strength of will and autonomy seem to be related. Will power would seem to be a natural outgrowth of autonomy.

𝕍 I should emphasize, though, that we are speaking only of the rudiments of will power at this level, and obviously not of mature will power. Only a mature person has will power in the full sense, but in the early stages, something fundamental develops without which the later mature human capacity cannot develop.

¶ So you are not talking about final character patterns at all. You're merely suggesting that the rudiments emerge here and continue to develop throughout these eight stages.

𝕍 Yes, they develop further in each stage as shown in my "epigenetic diagram."° They become more complex and differentiated, and therefore undergo renewed crises.

¶ At this point we might look at the use of the phrase "epigenetic diagram." You called these eight stages epigenesis, which is an interesting way to describe your developmental model.

𝕍 "Epi" means "upon"; and "genesis," "emergence." So epigenesis means that one item develops on top of another

---

° A detailed explanation and graphic presentation of the epigenetic psychosexual stages may be found in "The Theory of Infantile Sexuality," *Childhood and Society*, Chapter 2, pp. 48–108. A concise integration of the concepts discussed here, i.e. the relationship of the psychosexual stages to the psychosocial crises and resulting modalities, can be found in Erikson, "Identity and the Life Cycle: Selected Papers," in *Psychological Issues* [Monograph] (New York: International Universities Press, 1959), I, 1.

in space and in time, and this seemed to me a simple enough configuration to be adopted for our purposes. But, of course, I extended it to include a hierarchy of stages, not just a sequence.

¶ A question that is probably often asked you about these stages is the age of the child at these various stages. For instance, at what age does the oral-sensory stage develop in the child?

↜ I would say throughout the first year.

¶ And then the muscular-anal stage, the second one—when does it emerge?

↜ During the second and third year. But this differs in duration and intensity in different children and in different cultures.

¶ Cultural relativism would seem to be an important aspect of this pattern of development. In this respect you seem to be viewing psychosexual development from a slightly different perspective from Freud's. He wasn't quite as likely to say that these psychosexual levels would be different in different cultures, was he?

↜ I think that in his early work he was quite aware in an almost Marxian sense of differences, at least in different classes. But his, like any other scheme of stages, implies that the *sequence* could not be changed. And insofar as every human being is born as an organism, there are certain aspects in his development which remain universal, no matter where he grows up. The culture can only aggravate or play down, and in that way make the stages more or less intense, or more or less prolonged. And it can aggravate or smooth out the transitions. But what emerges is pretty much tied to what is fundamental to the psychosexual stages as well. Incidentally, it is also related to something we are not considering here at all, namely Piaget's stages of cognitive development.

Locomotor-Genital Stage: Initiative vs. Guilt / Purpose

¶ The cognitive, the psychosocial, and the psychosexual all play an important part in the model you have developed, then, and you have integrated all three into the epigenetic sequence. Now to return to our stage-by-stage discussion. The third stage, which would probably occur in our culture somewhere about two, three, or four years of age is the locomotor-genital stage. Here you talk about the characteristics of initiative versus guilt emerging from this level. The phallic stage in Freudian theory introduced the so-called Oedipal situation where the male child "falls in love" with the mother and the female child "falls in love" with the father and out of this, ideally for ego growth, the male child should identify with the father and develop a strong ego. You do not challenge the importance of the Oedipal situation in your particular approach, do you? For example, when you talk about initiative versus guilt, you are saying that these are out-growths of the Oedipal situations, are you not?

❦ Obviously we would not agree today with all the generalizations which have been made with regard to the Oedipus complex, least of all the female Oedipus complex. If you say that the little boy "falls in love" with his mother, and that later on he has trouble falling out of love with her, we must remember that from the beginning she was everything to the child. She was his first love "object" as analysis calls it. This is an unfortunate term, but Freud meant that drive needs an object, not that man needs other men as mere objects. The problem is that the mother becomes "naturally" involved in the boy's first genital fantasies, at a time when his whole initiative has to be and is ready to be deflected from the home and must find new goals. Immense new faculties develop in him at this time, and if his potentialities are permitted to develop fully, the child will be in much less danger of developing a severe complex. But I would think the Oedipus complex is more and less than what Freud made of it. From an evolutionary point of view, it is the ontogenetic way in which the human individual first experiences the inexor-able sequence of generations, of growth and of death.

¶ The particular virtue you see coming forth from all this is "purpose." Out of initiative, then, would develop some goal-directedness for the individual?

❦ Yes. The child begins to envisage goals for which his locomotion and cognition have prepared him. The child also begins to think of being big and to identify with people whose work or whose personality he can understand and appreciate. "Purpose" involves this whole complex of elements. For example, when the child plays, it's not just a matter of practicing his will or practicing his ability to manipulate. He begins to have projects, as it were. It is during this period that it becomes incumbent upon the child to repress or redirect many fantasies which developed earlier in his life. He begins to learn that he must work for things, and that even his secret wishes for omniscience and omnipotence must be attached to concrete things, or at least to things which can materialize. Paradoxically, he continues to feel guilty for his fantasies.

Latency Stage: Industry vs. Inferiority / Competence

¶ Having looked at the first three of the stages, Professor Erikson, let us discuss the next period, which you have termed latency, and where you introduce the traits of industry versus inferiority. This period in the child's life loosely parallels the period Freud also termed latency, but you have departed somewhat from the Freudian notion by introducing the parallel psychosocial traits, industry and inferiority. This is an interesting departure because Freud really gives very few clues as to what he felt was happening to the character development during this period. How does your model coincide with Freud's notion that the latency period involves a move from premature sexuality to a nonactive sexual level?

✷ Well, once you speak of the whole child, and not only of libido and defense, you have to consider that in each stage the child becomes a very different person, a person with increased cognitive capacities and a much greater ability to interact with a much wider range of people in whom he is interested, whom he understands, and who react to him. It would not be fair, in a way, to say that Freud did not consider this, because he was only concerned with the question of what happens to sexual energy during that time. To him, latency meant only that certain passionate and imaginative qualities of life are then relatively subdued, and the child is free to concentrate and learn. There is a lull during this period when sexuality must wait for puberty. In the meantime, the child learns the basic grammar, as it were, and the basic technology of his culture. The further psychoanalysis has changed its focus from an id psychology to an ego psychology, the clearer it has become that the ego can only remain strong in interaction with cultural institutions and can also only remain strong when the child's inborn capacities and potentials are developed. There is an enormous curiosity during this stage of life—a wish to learn, a wish to know. Piaget's work° permits us to bring the cog-

° See, for example, J. Piaget's *The Psychology of Intelligence* (London: Routledge and Kegan Paul, 1950).

nitive elements together with the psychosexual ones, for obviously learning is not just suppressed or displaced sexual curiosity; learning contains an energy of its own which Robert White [44] subsumes as a striving for competency. I agree with him that this is a fundamental, lifelong striving, but I would think that some experiential aspects of it undergo a special crisis in the "school" age.

¶ During the latency period, then, the polarities of industry versus inferiority are operating and the virtue of competence emerges.

𝕍 Yes. In deference to White, it might be better to speak of skill here. I would like to say another word about the history of psychoanalysis. In the early days we had observed in small patients of school age or in older patients who were fixated on it, that they showed not only an inhibition in learning but also a wish to go back to the basic family. Regressive pulls in human life were then much more emphasized than what pulls a child out of the past, out of the family and out to wider experiences. Every culture at this stage offers training and teaching. Indians out in the forest give a little boy a little play bow and arrow. We are a literate civilization and so we show children how to read and write. And there is a real revolution going on right now, which insists on new ways of introducing the child to a technological universe right from the beginning of school life.

¶ The latency period then is very important for industry, and when inferiority develops, it is because the child's attempts toward mastery have failed?

ℝ̌ Yes, his attempts toward specialized competence. The term "industry" is often misunderstood, because it now means "big" industry. Some people see red when I use simple terms which have been taken over into the ideology of mass production or banking. But the word "industry" belongs to everybody and really means industriousness, being busy with something, learning to complete something, doing a job—in the jungle or in the factory.

Adolescent Stage: Identity vs. Role Diffusion / Fidelity

¶ Then, moving on to the period which you call puberty or adolescence, around thirteen or fourteen years, you introduce the important psychosocial mechanisms of identity versus role diffusion. I think these concepts have given rise to some of the most intriguing observations in your work. Would you comment on these constructs *generally,* and on how you see this development through puberty and adolescence in particular?

ℝ̌ Since we first described identity as a relatively unconscious conflict, there has been something of an identity explosion. "Identity," and more surprisingly, "identity crisis," are words used all over the world with the connotations of professional identity, racial identity, national identity, and so on. Now, in my first book [10] I said that there were obvious cultural reasons why Freud, as a neurologist in the Victorian age, would have seen psycho-sexuality as the area in which human energies and resources were excessively repressed and misspent. But even where a person can adjust sexually in a technical sense and may at least superficially develop what Freud called genital maturity, he may still be weakened by the identity problems of our era. I would, in fact, add that it cannot develop without the development of a firm identity at the conclusion of adolescence. Maybe the fact that I am an immigrant to this country made me feel that the problem of identity holds a central position in the disturbances we encounter today. In other words, fully developed genitality is not a goal to be pursued in isolation. For here, immigrants first gave up old national identities on a gigantic scale for the sake of a new country and its tremendous industrial development. And the population is continually shifting and moving, socially and geographically. It's not only the first generation of Americans who face the problems of change, for they at least know where they came from and why they came. For the following generations apparently the problem of identity becomes a very central and disturbing one. This is *the* country of changes; it is obsessed with change. Others are taking over this pattern, and underdeveloped countries strive to achieve national identity by embracing change.

¶ The virtue which is developed at this stage is fidelity, is it not?

❦ Frankly, that term "virtue" comes like a shock to me every time it is mentioned. I should like to say something more about that. Many people are dubious of the attempt to tie anything which sounds like virtue or strength to an evolutionary process. This is a reaction, I suppose, against earlier attempts to show that the highest form of evolution is Christianity, or that the values of other systems are built into evolution. But I'm not speaking of values; I only speak of a developing capacity to perceive and to abide by values established by a particular living system. When I say "fidelity," I don't mean faith in a particular ideology, just as in using the word "hope" I don't mean a particular religious form of hope. If I could, I would differentiate between Hope with a capital "H" and hope with a small "h." Man is born only with the capacity to learn to hope, and then his milieu must offer him a convincing world view and within it specific hopes. I believe that these virtues are as necessary in human adaptation as instincts are among the animals. So, having reassured myself, I would go further and claim that we have almost an instinct for fidelity—meaning that when you reach a certain age you can and must learn to be faithful to some ideological view. Speaking psychiatrically, without the development of a capacity for fidelity the individual will either have what we call a weak ego, or look for a deviant group to be faithful to.

¶ The point you are making here is that adolescence is the phase specific to which identity or role confusion emerges, and that these are the basic ingredients of ego strength and development.

🦷 I think the potential for the development of ego strength comes out of the successful completion of all the earlier developmental processes. I would say that you could speak of a fully mature ego only after adolescence, which means, after all, becoming an adult. I've personally learned most from my work with children and with adolescents and young adults. As [August] Aichhorn has taught us, in working with late adolescents it isn't enough to interpret to them what went wrong in their past history. The present is too powerful for much retrospection. In fact, they often use that kind of interpretation to develop a florid ideology of illness, and actually become quite proud of their neuroses. Also, if everything "goes back" into childhood, then everything is somebody else's fault, and trust in one's power of taking responsibility for oneself may be undermined.

¶ Was this not satirized in the Broadway musical *West Side Story*, in the Officer Krupke song, where the ostensible juvenile delinquents were singing, "We're not responsible for our acts, social conditions are"? It amounts to a massive social rationalization mechanism. The poverty-stricken person says, "I'm not responsible for my poverty. It's society's fault." The delinquent says, "It's my mother's fault." This use of biological and social deterministic concepts may have led us backward rather than forward in many ways.

🔯 That's right. In fact, *West Side Story* has another very insightful theme. I don't remember the exact words, but these young people are dancing and singing, "They say we're bums. All right, that's what we're going to be." We meet something similar in other sections of rebellious youth. They tell us, "You say we have an identity crisis. All right, an identity crisis is what we're going to have." So what we once gingerly diagnosed as sexual identity confusion is now represented almost mockingly by otherwise rather wholesome-looking young people. This brings us back to the crux of the identity problem. I feel that our sense of identity is composed of both positive and negative elements. There are some things which we want to become, and we know we are supposed to be, and which —given good socio-historical situations—we can fulfill. Then there are things which we do not want to be or which we know we are not supposed to be. And then there are times which make it rather impossible for large groups of youth to be anything positive on a large and relevant scale, for example in the Nazi era.

¶ You speak about the negative and positive aspects of ego identity, and you have indicated that this is related to ideology, and since this seems to be a central aspect of your theory, I wonder if you would elaborate on that notion a bit.

🔯 The phenomenon has evolutionary as well as historical aspects. I would put it this way: Man has become divided into pseudo-species, and in the present era he is trying to overcome one of the last forms of pseudo-specieshood, namely nationalism. The tribal animal is on the defensive, just because more inclusive ideologies are being formed. Reactionary rage equipped with atomic weapons may mean the end of man just when for the first time he has a chance to become one species. But how to form a wider identity—that now becomes the problem of youth. Yet youth is only an intermediary stage of life in a given period of historical change. As I see it, the adolescent is driven and often disturbed by a new quantitive pressure of conflicting drives. So the ontogenetic aspect of adolescence is really representative of what each individual's ego strength must tackle at one and the same time, namely inner unruliness and changing conditions. Incidentally, I don't speak of ego strength as being merely defensive in nature. Anna Freud [19] has described the function of the ego as a bulwark against the quantity of drives. I think that this quantitative aspect of drive pressure depends very much on psychosocial development. A person whose potentialities as a person have no place in the historical trends of his time simply is more upset about what drives him amorphously, more inclined to regress and thus also more bothered with infantile remnants in his sexuality. You can see in any number of young people that they can take sexuality in their stride, can weather crises, and absorb some severe mistakes. So identity has that developmental importance. But then it also has its societal side, which is what makes it psychosocial. On the basis of cognitive development the young person is looking for an ideological framework by which to envisage a future of vast possibilities. It's very important to see that ideologies, by definition, cannot consist of mature values. Adolescents are easily seduced by totalitarian regimes and all kinds of totalistic fads which offer some transitory fake values, such as the Thousand-Year Reich which Hitler offered the German adolescents at a time when the Treaty of Versailles left them in despair.

¶ In your work on the Hitler regime and his rise to power, you were interested in the Hitler *Jugend,* and also your work on Maxim Gorky brought out the vulnerability of the adolescent.°

♔ Yes, vulnerability and strength at the same time, because you can see that while the adolescent is vulnerable to fake ideas, he can put an enormous amount of energy and loyalty at the disposal of any convincing system. This is what makes it so tragic and gives all creators of new values such responsibilities. We in the West pretend that we want to uphold only a "way of life," while in fact we too are creating and exporting technological and scientific ideologies, which have their own ways of enforcing conformity. The majority of our young adults gladly accept this as a basis for an identity of "what works is good." A minority of youth senses that what only "works" may be

---

° Erikson's discussion of Hitler and Gorky may be found in Chapters 9 and 10 respectively of *Childhood and Society* [10].

destructive unless restrained by a new sense of responsibility toward mankind as one species. These are two great sources of contemporary identity and identity confusion: faith in technology and a reassertion of a kind of humanism. Both are apt to be dated in their utopianism and inadequate for the gigantic struggle for man's mastery of his own powers.

¶ You seem to refer here to two levels of identity—one emerging in the biological developmental sequence, and the other tied to the psychosocial realm. In the latter case, you would say that an ideology then becomes a basis for identity.

👣 It doesn't have to be an ideology in the political sense, but an ideological framework, which is tuned to the need for new and more inclusive identities. Now, the problem of identity is that it must establish a continuity between society's past and future and that adolescence in all its vulnerability and power is the critical transformer of both. Let me go back to the epigenetic point of view. Identity develops through all earlier stages; it begins way back when the child first recognizes his mother and first feels recognized by her, when her voice tells him he is somebody with a name, and he's good. He already then begins to feel that he's somebody, he's an individual. But he has to go through many stages until he reaches the adolescent identity crisis. These stages I have not been able to describe yet. Mixed in with the positive identity, there is a negative identity which is composed of what he has been shamed for, what he has been punished for, and what he feels guilty about: his failures in competency and goodness. Identity means an integration of all previous identifications and self-images, including the negative ones. A boy may have loved an uncle who somehow became a derelict. It was made very clear to him that he must not be like that uncle, but the uncle is in him, juxtaposed to the images of the parents who may be "better" but only by unloving hypocrisy. Much of this goes on in the unconscious, of course, and it occurs to me that we have simply taken the unconscious for granted here. Let me pause to make this retroactive for everything we have said. Very important is the fact that the young (consciously or unconsiously) recognize their own negative identity in their parents, and begin to doubt whether earlier identifications with them are altogether as useful and admirable as previously thought. In other words, identity formation is really a restructuring of all previous identifications in the light of an anticipated future.

¶ To move to another aspect of the construct identity, I notice that Rokeach, in his recent book *The Three Christs of Ypsilanti* [38], gives some attention to your identity concept. In his particular scheme, he uses the term "primitive belief system," which is an attempt to look at the very fundamental conceptions of who one really is. These are such simple things that you learn, as your name, where you live and so on. During puberty and adolescence the developing individual gains some conception of where he is in this universe and that takes on fundamental meaning. Is this similar to what you're suggesting?

🐦 Yes. Psychosocial identity transcends mere "personal" identity, that is, the knowledge of who you are. Adolescence, as you can see all around us, most reconnects human past and human future. Puberty, as Anna Freud [19] has shown, produces a form of primitivity in thought and behavior. But I would not consider it all a defense, but rather a necessary reconnection of primitivity and modernity. Adolescents have always been especially open to conversion or to what is now called consciousness-expansion in the direction of physical, spiritual, and social experience. Their cognitive capacities and social interests are such that they want to go to the limit of experience before they fit themselves into their culture and fit their culture to themselves. In primitive cultures there are puberty rites which rather forcefully inform the growing youth where he belongs. He learns that he belongs to a particular tribe or a particular clan, and must pay the price of conformity for a sense of belongingness. Of course, the more a culture gives free choices and decisions as to who one is going to be, the more open conflict is aroused.

¶ In other words, the more highly structured a culture is, the less likely there will be an overt conflict of identity, while the less structure there is in a free society, the greater will be the conflict?

𝕎 I would think so. But, of course, it also means that wherever the identity is so preordained that you have fewer choices, there are fewer provisions for being somebody special or deviant or both. We would not know about the people in primitive tribes who fall by the wayside because they simply may not survive. In our society, we are witnessing a situation where youths sport an identity confusion very openly and almost mockingly, for they prefer to find their own way to new ethical commitments.

¶ As you have indicated earlier in our discussion about "identity crisis," this has become more and more part of the *Zeitgeist*. For example, the existentialists have talked a lot about this. Could you discuss in a bit more detail how you feel the identity crisis relates to positive and negative identity, and to the existentialist orientation?

𝕎 One could almost say that adolescents are transitory existentialists by nature because they become suddenly capable of realizing a separate identity. They therefore can feel not only involved in acute conflict but also very much isolated, a feeling which they are apt to totalize to the point of being preoccupied with premature wisdom and death or of being willing to sacrifice themselves for a cause, and sometimes for any escape from isolation and sense of restriction. I am not sure that much of popular existentialism is not an ideology permitting some (otherwise gifted people) to remain fanatic adolescents preoccupied with their isolation and therefore cut off from intimacy. You can see in the existentialist movies from Europe how an isolated position is cynically idealized. Camus, however, transcended this, for example in his story *L'Étranger* [6], *The Stranger*. A sudden alienation (another word used in much of the literature) is probably not avoidable and is possibly a creative factor in adolescence. It is stronger in some cultural situations than in others. At any rate, the integration of infantile part-identities and fragmentary roles can be interfered with by early frustration, by a schizoid sickness latent in the young person, by tragedies in the family, or by rapid social evolution or technological change. Given a quantity of sudden drives that become unmanageable, any combination of these can become critical. The adolescent may then take pride in being delinquent, ornery, dirty—and the majority "confirms" him by typing him with name-calling such as beatnik or Vietnik, or even peacenik, which can become a contemptible pastime. But let us not forget that the majority must reinforce their imagery, too, and the majority of youths today find their identity in technological civilization. As clinicians and intellectuals (and maybe aesthetes), we know more about the dissenters.

¶ When one looks at this from the point of view of social psychology, it sometimes appears as if a delinquent youngster, in rebelling against the conformist pressure of so-called conventional society, has become a conformist in a delinquent subculture. So an escape to this "deviant subculture" from conformist demands of conventional society isn't an escape from conformity at all, is it?

❦ For the longest time we have failed to see that the delinquent adolescent, too, is looking for the chance to conform to some subculture, to be loyal to some leader, and to display and develop some kind of fidelity. We cannot treat them as the police and courts often do, as "naturally" inferior people with exclusively negative values. There are very few really bad people in the world, and I think they can be found rather among those who misuse youth. Those who become delinquent have simply been sidetracked because we failed them, and if we fail to recognize this fact, we lose them.

¶ I wonder if you might have some observations on the notion of positive and negative identity as a recurring problem for the person as he moves through adolescence toward maturity and old age. You seem to imply that it recurs again and again throughout the life of man.

❦ Yes, this is an intriguing subject. Before we get to it, let me again say something about the one-stage-after-another approach which you have employed in your questioning. This may be unavoidable, but it misses the nature of epigenetic stages in which each stage adds something specific to all later ones, and makes a new ensemble out of all the earlier ones. Identity does not first emerge in youth and it is not the aim and end of development. Our times emphasize identity as a predominant concern. If the relation of father and son dominated the last century, then this one is concerned with the self-made man asking himself what he is making of himself. Yet, this cannot be the last question. So I am glad that you lead me beyond the adolescent stage and our culture's fixation on it. You are right that even though one has resolved his identity crisis, later changes in life can precipitate renewal of the crisis. Maybe as an immigrant (and—as I indicated earlier—I had changed nationalities before as a small child) I faced one of those very important redefinitions that a man has to make who has lost his landscape and his language, and with it all the "references" on which his first sensory and sensual impressions, and thus also some of his conceptual images, were based. Migration can do that. As you have said, old age can do it, too, because the person who has not adequately solved his identity problem earlier will frantically try to see whether he can still develop another identity. His life is not quite acceptable to him as the only life he will ever have. People who know how to write autobiographies can create a retrospective identity, of course.

¶ By the way, is this not the focus of the study you did on *Young Man Luther* [8]?

❦ Yes, it is. But it will be more explicit in my discussion of Gandhi's more formal autobiography [13].

¶ Luther's whole problem of identity was dealt with in your book as it was established in adolescence and continued to be an important problem even after he became an innovator in a religious movement.

❦ Luther was a very troubled and a very gifted young man who had to create his own "cause" on which to focus his fidelity in the Roman Catholic world as it was then. As you know, he first became a monk and tried to solve his scruples by being an exceptionally good monk. But even his superiors thought that he tried much too hard. He felt himself to be such a sinner that he began to lose faith in the charity of God, and his superiors told him, "Look, God doesn't hate you; you hate God or else you would trust Him to accept your prayers." But I would like to make it clear that someone like Luther becomes an historical person only because he also has an acute understanding of historical actuality and knows how to "speak to the condition" of his times. Only then do inner struggles become representative of those of a large number of vigorous and sincere young people—and begin to interest some troublemakers and hangers-on.

¶ Another current area of discussion relating to the problem of identity in a broad sense deals with the female in our culture. Freud, of course, reflecting the difficulties of the female child in resolving the Oedipal situation, seemed to view the female as being destined to a basic immaturity throughout her life. In view of the increased possibilities for fulfillment and education for women today, we might raise the question of whether Freud's analysis remains valid or whether it was another example of his alleged culture-bound perception, possibly influenced by the female of his era. Do you view the female identity problem in a manner different from that of Freud?

♈ My feeling is that Freud's general judgment of the identity of women was probably the weakest part of his theory. Exactly what is to blame for that I don't know, except that he was a Victorian man, a patriarchal man. He may have missed the whole substratum of matriarchy in man. Also, he was a doctor, and he obviously saw in his women patients what you first get in the free association of any patients, namely, the story of deprivation and resentment. And finally, it probably took a certain development of the field, including the participation of women doctors, to help men to empathize with women—a dangerous undertaking for a man if your public role, your preferred method, and your masculine identity all depend on each other. The point is not to deny what Freud saw and generalized. For there can be no doubt that women in many ways envy masculinity deeply. Any little girl growing up at that time, or, for that matter, throughout the patriarchal era of mankind, could see that a boy, just because of his anatomical appendage, was considered more important. That behind man's insistence on male superiority there is an age-old envy of women who are sure of their motherhood while man can be sure of his fatherhood only by restricting the female, that is another matter. At any rate, psychoanalytic literature tends to describe woman as an essentially passive and masochistic creature, who not only accepts the roles or "identity" assigned to her submissively, but needs all the masochism she can muster to appreciate the phallic male. But I would think that passive and masochistic are relative terms. Basically, the female anatomy suggests different modes of activity, within which a woman can be very active indeed, or very passive, and even very active in playing passive. Freud's perception might also have been colored by the sexual mores of his time, which could not admit at first that an upper-class woman could have passionate and active sexual wishes and yet be refined and intelligent. She had to act a bit as if something terrible was happening to her. You may remember that it was the anemic woman who was supposed to be the most "feminine." At the same time, the evaluation of childbearing in the culture of Freud's era was slanted toward considering it a more animalistic activity, one that needed less brains, and could be less easily sublimated into "higher" strivings. All of this most women had, in fact, accepted. So you are right: women could not help harboring that inner rage which comes from having to identify with your exploiters' negative image of you. And, as usual, the exploiter offered some complex compensation in his own terms, offering (to high and low) the ideal of the lady, or the keeper of the house, or the courtesan. Given such different roles the question is always what single role or what combination of several roles can lead to a sense of being fulfilled as a person.

¶ How do you feel about the resistance in this country to the movement of the female into more or less traditional male roles as has happened in the Soviet Union? For instance, some 70 percent of the physicians and dentists in the Soviet Union are female, as against a very small percentage in this country.

❦ Among the Soviet, I understand that the ratio of women doctors is a reflection of a more general population problem. During the war the Russians needed all the manpower they could muster, and after the war, they had lost so many well-trained men that they put the women to work wherever they felt they could work well. But it is interesting that they did not hesitate to think women would make good doctors, and even good surgeons, without being less women. I hear from Russian friends, however, that Russian men still hesitate to cook and to do the dishes, so a woman surgeon may have a second job on her hands when she comes home, even though her husband may have sat in an office all day. Elsewhere, the first generation of women who broke into traditional masculine occupations had to develop a kind of mannish competitiveness which was then held against them. The male doctors themselves forced the female doctors to become pseudo-men. So the big question is, Can women, after they have been admitted to full partnership in certain activities and after they have shown that in many essentials they can do fully as well as men, still use their new knowledge in order to contribute something to their fields as women? Many women consider this suggestion—that women may yet contribute something specifically feminine to so-far masculine fields—only a new form of discrimination. Yet there is a sudden general awareness which has gripped this country in the last few years that something is yet missing in American women's emancipation. Quite recently, President Johnson has declared that he wants women in government both for their ability and in order to bring some feminine influence to bear on that sphere. But, as you suggest, perhaps even the first round of emancipation has not been won here. We have, I believe, fewer women in Congress and in science than have, say, Germany, Japan, and India. Beyond that, my general position is that, man or woman, we have no right to foreclose the matter by assuming that women once truly emancipated and fully competent may *not* have some new directions to offer. As a man living in the nuclear age, I can only hope they do.

¶ Do you think that there is a possibility that what we have culturally defined as femininity and masculinity will disappear? Perhaps the time will come when simply saying that the female is a pseudo-male is an irrelevant point. Do you think we may eventually get to greater unity and look at the individual as an individual regardless of whether the person is male or female, thus allowing for greater individual development of identity?

⚘ I would think that what we need is a hierarchy of differences. For example, I think that in problems of individuality and selfhood a man and a woman are much more alike than in anything else, though, of course, never the same, for individuality is tied to a body. On the other hand, there are aspects of the body—as I mentioned earlier—in which women are basically so different from men that the feminine ego has a very specific task to perform in integrating body, role, and individuality. What I dislike about some psychological tests is that they compare the occurrence of a given item in women and in men, rather than assigning to such an item a place in the total configuration of womanhood or manhood. For example, it may be that woman has a finer touch, a finer sense of texture, finer discrimination for certain noises, a better memory for most immediate experience, a greater capacity to empathize immediately and emotionally, while the man may rate less in all of that. Does that make the woman "more aesthetic," the man less so? The point is: in a man, all of this would make him more aesthetic than most men; in a woman such "aesthetic" giftedness may be part of a total configuration which makes her a better mother of a number of children, one of whom may be a baby and one an adolescent, not to mention her husband. She has to empathize, in one day, with totally different joys and calamities, needs and sicknesses. Or the man may be "more muscular" than the woman and therefore judged to be "stronger," while she has the hips to bear twins and later to carry one on each hip. So who can say which is "stronger" and which is "weaker"?[*]

Young Adulthood Stage: Intimacy vs. Isolation—Love

¶ Now, moving to the next stage in your epigenetic cycle which you refer to as young adulthood, here you introduce intimacy versus isolation. This would appear to refer to the individual who, having grown beyond the beginnings of dealing with his identity problem, can move toward the issue of relationships with others. Is this what you're suggesting?

Of course, I mean something more—I mean intimate relationships, such as friendship, love, sexual intimacy, even intimacy with oneself, one's inner resources, the range of one's excitements and commitments. Intimacy is really the ability to fuse your identity with somebody else's without fear that you're going to lose something yourself. It is this development of intimacy which makes marriage possible as a chosen bond. When this has not

[*] Erikson's further reflections on womanhood may be found in Robert J. Lifton (ed.), *The Woman in America* (Boston: Houghton Mifflin, 1965), pp. 1–26.

developed, marriage is meaningless. But, of course, sometimes the inner development waits for the formal bond.

¶ This is consistent with findings of the sociologists that early marriages characteristically are not as stable as are marriages between older persons.

☞ Many young people marry in order to find their identity in and through another person, but this is difficult where the very choice of partner was made to resolve severe unconscious conflict. To be really intimate a rather firm identity has to be at least in the making. All this is a little more complicated with women because women, at least in yesterday's cultures, had to keep their identities incomplete until they knew their man. Yet, I would think that a woman's identity develops out of the very way in which she looks around and selects the person with whose budding identity she can polarize her own. Her selection is already an expression of her identity, even if she seems to become totally absorbed in somebody else's life.

¶ You feel, then, that the individual must be pretty well prepared in young adulthood to assume the responsibility and intimacy of marriage?

☞ Certainly. But I don't want to sound too moralistic about it. When I say intimacy, I do not mean intimacies. Obviously, adolescents as well as young adults, before they are able to develop true intimacy, may experiment in many ways with intimacies now increasingly sanctioned by custom. But I would think that they often experiment just because they have observed that institutional constraints did not guarantee true intimacy in their parents.

¶ Then there is a possibility of a pseudo-intimacy at the earlier stages of adolescence which may be mistaken for real intimacy. The traits you stress in connection with the young adult stage which comes after adolescence are intimacy versus isolation and the virtue here is love. This is really the beginning of what we call the mature, unselfish kind of love. This would be sharply different from the "love" discussed by Freud in the Oedipal situation.

ᏤϞ You're right, if you mean that here, too, he was merely concerned with freeing the adult capacity to love from infantile remnants.

Adulthood Stage: Generativity vs. Stagnation / Care

¶ And in the next stage, which is adulthood, you say that adulthood begins to deal with generativity versus stagnation. The individual presumably takes his place in society-at-large.

ᏤϞ Yes. At this stage one begins to take one's place in society, and to help in the development and perfection of whatever it produces. And one takes responsibility for that. I know that generativity is not an elegant word, but it means to generate in the most inclusive sense. If I would call this strength creativity, I would put too much emphasis on the particular creativity which we ascribe to particular people. I use the word "generativity" because I mean everything that is generated from generation to generation: children, products, ideas, *and* works of art.

¶ Then a person could be "generating" by making a contribution appropriate to his particular potential, even though he isn't a Mozart or a Picasso. For example, could a good mother be exhibiting generativity?

🦷 Yes, but even without having children, provided an individual can bear the unavoidable frustration. It is possible for a person to fulfill his generativity by working with other people's children or helping to create a better world for them. Women especially, but not exclusively, are apt to feel that they are frustrated in something essential if they do not produce children. But with the world's plans for population control, it is important for us to support the idea that a person can be generative by helping to create a world which can promise a minimum to every child born. That would include not only survival and subsistence, but also the development of the strengths we are talking about here. But one also has to understand the frustration implicit in limiting fertility, even as Freud showed us the devastating results of frustrations in genitality.

¶ I gather that you have so far avoided referring specifically to genital-creative levels of development because they have been too strictly interpreted by some orthodox psychoanalytical theories as sublimated sexuality, rather than emphasizing how genital-creative levels transcend the earlier sexual developmental pattern.

🖝 I would go even further than that and say that Freud, by paying so much attention to the prepubertal impediments of the genital encounter itself, underemphasized the procreative drive as also important to man. I think this is a significant omission, because it can lead to the assumption that a person graduates from psychoanalytic treatment when he has been restored to full genitality. As in many movies, where the story ends when lovers finally find one another, our therapies often end when the person can consummate sexuality in a satisfactory, mutually enriching way. This is an essential stage but I would consider generativity a further psychosexual stage, and would postulate that its frustration results in symptoms of self-absorption.

¶ The virtue which you propose to accompany the notion of generativity versus self-absorption in adulthood is care. Superficially, the productive connotation of this dichotomy is clear, but the concept of care seems to be somewhat inconsistent with the model of creativity. Would you clarify for us what you mean by the term "care" in this regard?

🐚 I needed one word and of all the words that I considered, I thought "care" was the strongest. Since I was not "born to the English language," the dictionary must be my companion, but usage must also be considered. Care originally meant an anxious kind of solicitude, but I think it has taken on more positive connotations. I use "care" in a sense which includes "to care to do" something, to "care for" somebody or something, to "take care of" that which needs protection and attention, and "to take care not to" do something destructive.

Old Age and Maturity Stage: Ego Integrity vs. Despair / Wisdom

¶ Your final stage is old age and maturity. You have counterposed ego integrity versus despair, with wisdom being the virtue of this period. This aspect of man may become even more important in the future as the life span is increased, and the fields of geriatrics and gerontology receive more attention. Have you given more consideration to this period since you first envisioned it?

🐚 I'm not satisfied with the term "wisdom," because to some it seems to mean a too-strenuous achievement for each and every old person. It is also perfectly obvious that if we live long enough, we all face a renewal of infantile tendencies—a certain childlike quality, if we're lucky, and senile childishness, if we're not. The main point is again a developmental one: only in old age can true wisdom develop in those who are thus "gifted." And in old age, *some* wisdom *must* mature, if only in the sense that the old person comes to appreciate and to represent something of the "wisdom of the ages," or plain folk "wit."

¶ In a sense, then, what you are calling wisdom is the embodiment of all these eight stages.

🕊 Yes, but it also means that you have to be able, in old age, to renounce some of the earlier things, because you can't be very wise if you still try to capture what you had or did not have as a youth.

The Epigenetic Framework and Possible Relationships to Psychopathology

¶ Perhaps we can conclude this portion of our discussion of your eight stages of man by asking you to respond briefly to some questions which I believe represent a particularly difficult challenge. The most difficult application of any developmental model is to relate symptoms of emotional disturbance appearing later in the life of an individual to earlier stages represented in the model. Might we look at your developmental model as a basis for analysis of acute emotional disturbances such as a psychosis?

❦ Let's not tackle such a massive problem as an *acute* psychosis. However, we do find in potentially psychotic people that the very first relationships in earliest childhood seem to have been severely disturbed. We could speak here of a psychosocial weakness which consists of a readiness to mistrust and to lose hope in rather fundamental ways. I do see the aggravation of basic mistrust as one of the conditions which induces the psychotic to "break off with reality." This could underlie a latent malignancy. Someday, I suppose, we will even understand the physiological substratum of hope. In the meantime, you remember that Frieda Fromm-Reichmann was a doctor who doggedly sat down with psychotics as if saying, "I'm not going to give up until you trust again." She felt that some psychotics must restore that one-to-one relationship which is the original source of hope in infancy, in order to trust the world again. This is as complex as it sounds simple, yet some of our untrained college students spontaneously understand this feat and learn to take time off from their hyperintellectual studies just to sit with a psychotic stranger on some state hospital ward. Frankly, such bravery restores my hope even where it does not always restore the patient's. But I would think that another useful way of employing my developmental model would be an attempt to specify for each stage what seemingly malignant kinds of disturbance may be treatable as an aggravated development crisis rather than as lastingly malignant. This is very important clinically. For it might keep us from confirming a patient as "a psychotic" who has transitory psychotic-like symptoms during an acute crisis.

¶ We find that schizophrenia often manifests itself in adolescence or late adolescence. Do you see a parallel between the identity crisis of adolescence and the onset of a disorder such as schizophrenia?

♈ Oh, decidedly so. But as I said, to understand this as part of a life crisis may reduce the fatalism of some diagnoses.

¶ Would you feel also that a psychotic disorder such as paranoia, which is quite rare, and usually occurs about middle age, might be related to the problems of developing intimacy and generativity, as you have postulated in the developmental sequence for the age of maturity and old age?

♈ Insofar as my developmental scheme contains a diagnostic one, I would differentiate between a period of fixation in childhood and periods of developmental arrest in later life. For example, a person might have been fixated somewhere between the hope and the will state—he has never quite overcome an early suspicion that the people who were allegedly trying to train his will were really trying to break it. This can remain a deep-seated mistrust, and the person remains somewhat estranged from his own will as well as that of others. Yet throughout his life all this may remain relatively dormant because of a certain capacity to utilize opportunities constructively. But when the individual's capacities and opportunities deteriorate in later life, he may reach a stage of arrest, beyond which he does not seem to be able to adjust. He may come to mistrust the whole world as conspiring to dominate his will, feeling that they are "after him," and he may even suspect his own inner voice and project it on voices he hears speaking to him. But this explains only a certain psychosocial predisposition to paranoia.

¶ How might you relate extreme obsessive-compulsive behavior to your developmental model?

♈ It would fit in where compulsion and obsession and impulsion, if you permit the word, would also be symptoms of a badly integrated will, although the compulsive person would be tormented more by guilt than by shame. He overcontrols himself because his will does not seem firm enough in relaxation. He must ritualize his self-control. He lacks the resilient self-will with which a mature person can make himself adhere to a certain order and yet also break that order at times. Such a character fixation may have its roots in early experiences and remain relatively well integrated with opportunities which call for some compulsiveness. But it may become unbearably aggravated in later crises. Therapeutically, it is important to see that the cure would lie not only in the clarification of the past drives which had to be held in check so rigidly but also in the support of present developmental powers: for every developmental crisis brings with it not only increased vulnerabilities but also *some* new strength.

2. Cross-Cultural and Psycho-Historical Analyses

Observations of "Primitive" Cultures, the Sioux and the Yurok

¶ DR. EVANS: Two of your especially unique and innovative contributions center around your interest in cross-cultural and what you refer to as psycho-historical analyses. Among the significant contributors to psychoanalysis, none, in my opinion, have made a more ingenious use of such analyses. It would be interesting to learn how you, as a psychoanalyst, happened to become interested in cross-cultural observation.

🖝 PROFESSOR ERIKSON: I must confess again that such decisive matters often happen quite by accident, and one knows only afterward that one happened to take the next step needed in the history of one's field. Actually, I just indulged myself in a new interest shared with a friend. In the middle thirties, I met an anthropologist, Scudder Mekeel (you probably have never heard of him; he died very young), who was field representative of the Commissioner of Indian Affairs. He suggested that I go with him to the Sioux Indians and take a look at their children and their schools, which were primarily staffed by non-Indians, in fact, often by Easterners. The childhood of these children, or indeed, the traditional upbringing of children in their tribe, was not being taken into account then, and Mekeel felt that I might be helpful in getting such inquiries started. When I realized (it took me some time) that Sioux is the name which in Europe we pronounced "See-ux," and which for us was *the* "American Indian," I could not resist. There was a German author, Karl May, who wrote many books about the Plains Indians which we as boys had read avidly.

¶ Your work with the Sioux became the basis for a good many very fascinating observations, which you wrote about in *Childhood and Society* [10]. It would be interesting to know what kinds of techniques you used to study them. For example, I know that cultural anthropologists have used what we call participant observation. How do you feel about this approach?

❦ I like the term "participant observation" because it makes clear that in any observation of human beings, you are also a participant, and must include your participation in your "design." I feel, incidentally, that we must also develop the capacity to become observant participants in areas such as politics; that is, we must be willing to participate without sacrificing insight. With the Indians, of course, I had to rely very heavily on my friend. In this study, as well as in one I did in California with Alfred Kroeber, the anthropologist knew the tribe very well and had become friends with some of the old people in the tribes. On the borderline of their studies they had been left with questions which were also on the borderline of mine. They took me to the field and introduced me to the old informants and said, "You treat this man the way you treated me, and tell him what you would have told me." The two anthropologists were so beloved by some older people in these particular tribes that to some extent I could just "step in." Without that initial assistance, I could never have done my work. Also, these anthropologists had collected a great amount of data, some of it unpublished, which I could study in advance. And I had had intensive conversations with Margaret Mead. As to the Sioux, the government had published a three-hundred-page handbook. Only half a page of it was devoted to childhood training. And yet, it was the easiest thing in the world to go out there and ask the grandmothers, "Now, before the white man came, how were your children brought up?" They loved to talk about it, and they had always wondered why on earth nobody had ever asked them.

¶ As a pioneer child analyst, did not this opportunity to study these Indian cultures open a new horizon of investigation for you, in that it allowed cross-cultural "tests" of psychoanalytic hypotheses?

Not only that. The interesting thing was that all the childhood problems which we had begun to take seriously on the basis of pathological developments in our own culture, the Indians talked about spontaneously and most seriously without any prodding. They referred to our stages as the decisive steps in the making of a good Sioux Indian or a good Yurok Indian. What we describe clinically as orality and anality, the Indians evaluated and emphasized according to whether these characteristics would serve to develop the kind of person the culture considered "good." And "good" meant whatever seemed "virtuous" in a "strong" man or woman in that culture. I think this contributed eventually to my imagery of basic human strengths.

¶ So, you apparently began to look at this Sioux culture, which has a lesser degree of technological development than ours, and you could see a pattern of child development which could contribute insights bearing on your eight stages of man. After you saw that this would be a good vehicle for study, how did you attempt to analyze the differences between the Sioux culture and Western society?

🐚 Actually, I evolved the eight stages later, partially as a result of bringing the observations on Indians back to our own culture. First of all, I found that what Freud had described as pregenital stages were also important as precultural stages intrinsically related to the technology and the world image of a culture. That was a basic, new insight then. The eight stages of man were really formulated for the White House Conference of 1950. The planners of that conference challenged us, who had looked at children for so long, to tell them how "normality" develops. So I charted the stages of a "healthy" personality, but I kept the word "healthy" in quotation marks.

¶ After the full impact of orthodox Freudian theory began to be felt, about the 1920's, some cultural anthropologists, such as Malinowski [30], went into the field to determine the universality of some of Freud's concepts. Some of their early findings appear to challenge at least some of Freud's notions. Would that be a fair interpretation?

🐚 As far as I can remember, Malinowski challenged the existence of a latency period, but he did not challenge Freud's infantile sexual stages. In fact, he tried to show that where you have primitivity you have no genital repression, because he observed children in the latency period indulging in sex play. However, one could interpret Malinowski's material differently. For instance, sex play could be primarily "funny" role play with little sexual involvement. In fact, children laugh when they are involved in it. The very fact of such overt freedom could make the taboos even more sinister.

Hitler's National Socialism / a Psycho-Historical Analysis

¶ Now to move to a different but somewhat related area of your interests, as you studied the human development cycle of different cultures in an attempt to find data bearing on your theoretical framework, you have also explored historically and written about the German culture and the Gorky pattern [10]. You also analyzed, as we briefly discussed earlier, historical influences which manifested themselves in Martin Luther [8]. Then recently you did some work in India [13]. I wonder if you might share with us a few of the insights you have gained from these various analyses and observations.

First of all, I have indeed been in India recently to study the traditional version of the life cycle there. But your question leads us back to before I came to this country. I was in Vienna when Hitler came to power in Germany. Luckily (in every way) I had married an American girl, and we had already decided to move to this country. On the boat coming over, I sat down to write out a few things I felt were decisive in turning German youths toward Hitler. In the cabin next to us was a man named George Kennan, with his family. He was then (I think) Third Secretary of the American Embassy in Moscow. You are familiar with the role he played later in American foreign policy. We started talking, and he was deeply concerned about the German situation. So when he heard what I was trying to write with my few hundred words of "Basic English," he said, "Why don't we translate your German notes into English together?" So on the deck of that boat I had George Kennan's help in writing out the notes which later became the chapter on Hitler in my book *Childhood and Society* [10]. But my original purpose was really to explain this phenomenon to myself. I had gone to school in Germany. I myself was born a Dane, but the German language had become my language and the German countryside my first "milieu" as an artist. These German youths had turned Nazi and were, in fact, killing off some of my Jewish friends. They might have disposed of me if I had been there. I felt then, and feel strongly now, what Hannah Arendt [3] pointed out, that one has no right to consider this simply a criminal interlude in history, the criminals always being the "others." That the potentialities for such destruction are in decent and cultured people is something we have to account for. Or rather, we have to study it, psycho-historically, as I would say today. Hitler was a young man with much stored-up rage within him because of his unfulfilled potentials. So was Luther. Some of my friends have not forgiven me for writing about young Hitler as one who at one time, too, wanted to rebuild, as a young person with potentialities that might have gone in a number of directions. The main object of psycho-historical investigations is to try to relate the particular identity-needs of a given leader to the "typical" identity-needs of his historical time. The solution he finds for himself becomes prototypical of the solution for the young people of his time. If criminality on a large scale results, then the whole adult generation must take the responsibility for not having provided other viable opportunities for the young. Post–World War I was such a period in Germany. Hitler was certainly driven by "insane" motivations. But only by an historical coincidence of his own deranged fate and the fate of many youths in his nation did he become representative of the negative identity of Germany, and could bring his evil genius into play. Everything that the world had always criticized as "German," the Nazis made to appear positive and pretended that it was what they really wanted to be.

¶ Are you saying that the national character, the existing stereotype of the German, became incorporated in the feelings of the people, and became in fact a sort of self-fulfilling prophecy? That the Germans in fact *became* what they were most *supposed* to be—aggressive, power-seeking, without conscience?

More than that. Hitler would go so far as to say, "Conscience is a blemish like circumcision." In other words, traditional Judaeo-Christian values now became negative self-images and were projected onto the Jews. I call this phenomenon a totalistic split which happens in world history when a group or nation cannot fulfill its positive potentials. It happens in delinquents, as we discussed earlier. When they cannot find a form for their adolescent powers, they may be driven to despair, to making a totalistic choice, and to accepting a negative identity rather than a positive one that would be fragmentary at best. When you face a defiant delinquent who seems quite unapproachable and who seems to have no conscience at all, you may be sure that you are dealing with such a totalistic split.

¶ Under normal conditions, then, there is a spectrum from which the developing person could manifest one or another of a wide variety of possibilities. But in extreme circumstances, a kind of polarization is the result, and the person becomes one of the two extremes of his potential. You are saying that the world of a deviant youngster may force such a polarization on him, even as it might affect an anger-ridden man like Hitler. The question is, then: What causes some people to react in a negative fashion and others to choose a less extreme form of reaction to similarly unhealthy conditions?

To answer that, I might go back a moment to the question as to why Hitler failed. Is his failure the only evidence for the argument that he was bad? I'm sure some

Germans today still feel that his only mistake was that his plans didn't work. Yet, could they possibly have worked? I think that there was really no possibility for their fulfill-ment in long-range actuality. I do not think that his ideas ever had a chance to activate a future. Preoccupation with death and destructiveness rather than "love of life" do not appear to go hand in hand with a constructive future.

¶ The term Erich Fromm gives to this reaction is necro-philia,° a pathological preoccupation with such death and destructiveness. Would this description relate to yours?

I don't know how far Fromm goes with that kind of analysis. He may be overstating this and, strangely enough, reviving the logic of Freud's "death instinct." But I may mean the same thing when I say that when future growth becomes unfulfillable, a deep rage is aroused in man comparable to that of an animal driven into a corner —only that man's instinctual arousals and suppressions of all kinds reinforce each other and become independent of "instinctive" purposes and situations. So only man can be "necrophilic," and can mask his rage with moral indigna-tion. On the other hand, the love of life cannot be en-forced by injunction or persuasion. Love of life can only

° Note that Fromm's definition of necrophilia differs from the one which relates this concept to a particular sexual deviancy. See R. I. Evans, *Dialogue with Erich Fromm* (New York: Harper & Row, 1966), pp. 11–12.

win out where developing potentialities are given a chance of realization.

¶ Would you feel that the development of this kind of pattern today could produce similar dictators? Are we likely to produce more Hitlers?

❦ I suppose that comparable and yet dissimilar historical situations are always possible. So we must learn to anticipate entirely new dangers in new settings. But let me turn to another aspect of your earlier question. The other day I spoke about Gandhi and nonviolence in my son's seminar at Emory University in Atlanta. Margaret Mead was visiting, and she asked what, in my terms, the difference was between a Gandhi and a Hitler. That's an interesting question, which cannot be answered on the basis of the fact that most of us like the one and not the other.

¶ Can we say that the leader emerges as an embodiment of the character of a nation, and is positively or negatively shaped according to its national character? Might a Khrushchev or a Johnson, for instance, once in power, be shaped according to this "national identity"?

❦ I think I would have to differentiate here between ideological rebels and innovators and leaders who are more like the caretakers of their nation's existing development. With the group whom I call ideological innovators, the personal life history and personal conflicts are more determining. But to stay within our discourse: the best leader is the one who realizes what potentials can be activated in those led, and most of all, what more inclusive identities can be realized. Since you mention him, I would think that Lyndon Johnson is up to a point such a leader, to the surprise of some people. He personifies something that a wide segment of the American population can identify with, including even sections of the Negro world, because he includes them. But whether he understands the new and more inclusive identities emerging in the rest of the world among peoples long deprived of their potentials, that is another and possibly tragic question.

¶ I imagine the manner in which a leader rises to power is related to this.

🐦 Yes. There are some leaders who surprise us totally because they appear suddenly out of nowhere or what we thought was nowhere. Hitler, for years, was absolutely nobody. Two years of his life are altogether unaccounted for. Gandhi always insisted that he wanted to be "zero," and he deliberately identified himself with the lowest strata of the Indian population. Then he became a leader without assuming any kind of conventional power. But he was a master in molding existing potentialities together. That they fell apart again, and literally with a vengeance, that must be studied, too.

¶ It would seem that they were each attempting to reach certain goals which represent certain kinds of power, and that one used techniques of violence, while the other used nonviolence.

☙ That is true, but it is not the whole point either. Nonviolence cannot in itself be the point, because great leaders whom some of us would continue to consider great have considered the use of violence and even of nuclear violence necessary, or not yet expendable. But in the meantime, I would repeat that the best leader is the one who can realize the actual potentials in his nation, and most of all the more inclusive identities which are ready to be realized in the world. That, at least, excludes small wars, or uses them only to confirm larger identities. The difference between a Hitler and a Gandhi is (in this context) that Hitler's violent methods were tied to a totalistic reinforcement of a pseudo-species (the German race), the fiction of which could only be maintained by vilifying and annihilating another pseudo-subspecies, the Jews. Gandhi's nonviolent technique, on the contrary, was not only tied to the political realities of his day, but also revived the more inclusive identity promised in the world religions.

Gandhi's Nonviolence / Philosophy and Technique

¶ It would be interesting to learn if one of your interests in India was to identify the source of the protest mechanism which Gandhi employed in the form of nonviolence.

Dialogue with Erik Erikson

☞ It was not initially my intention to study Gandhi and nonviolence as a technique of protest when I went to India. While I was working in the city of Ahmedabad, I met a number of Gandhi's old friends and adversaries who were with him at a critical event in his ascent to national leadership, an event which I had dimly read about when I was young. I realized that here I could "get at" an historical event by interviewing people who had participated in it. Also Gandhi was fifty years old at that time. As my students put it: "Erikson wrote a book on *Young Man Luther* [8], so now he must write a book on 'Middle-Aged Mahatma.'" In 1918, you see, Gandhi was one of a number of mahatmas; Indian history is full of mahatmas. But then he became *the* Mahatma through a number of events. The event I have been trying to reconstruct [11] was his intervention in a mill strike in the city of Ahmedabad, one of the most concentratedly industrial towns in India. Two things stimulated my old interest in Gandhi. For one, he now seemed to me to exemplify in word and deed what I had come to perceive as a modern version of the golden rule. To put it briefly, this version suggests that wherever one has a choice one should choose to act so as to enhance the potentials of one's counterplayer's development as well as one's own. Maybe we can discuss this later. I know of no other example in world history where a man made such a principle so completely his own by always extending it to his opponent. This became clear as I heard more and more about that event. Gandhi had agreed to take over the leadership of the mill workers if they would promise to help him create a situation in which both the mill workers and the mill owners would emerge as more mature human beings. This ethical principle was, of course, entirely embedded in economic problems: Gandhi never divorced "lofty" matters from the most concrete ones, including "dirty" politics. Even today that city has the best labor relations of any city in India, although some critics are probably right who feel that Gandhi's solutions, too, were bound to their period, and were antirevolutionary.

¶ Comparing the techniques of *violence* which emerged under Hitler in Germany and those of *nonviolence* in Gandhi's India, there must be some profound cultural differences which account for the emergence of such dramatic differences in the techniques of leadership which the people will tolerate.

☞ No doubt, there is a long cultural development which makes it historically plausible that "nonviolence" first was systematized in India. But then the historical problem is the convergence of a life history like Gandhi's with an historical trend, and the resulting actualization of a new direction. Gandhi wrote a detailed autobiography [23], which is a great help for an analyst, although he must be careful not to read a man's literary confessions as though they were free associations [13]. Great confessions are always part self-revelation, part "propaganda." But I also find it fascinating to study what happened in the lives of the followers I'm interviewing. Why and how did Gandhi suddenly become so important to them? Why were they ready for him? How did he draw out of them the strength they displayed in serving him? Why did Gandhi choose these then young people and how did he know what roles to assign to them? And what was it in Indian history that would make Indians feel that nonviolence might be the weapon that would give them self-respect and would help them to meet a superior enemy head-on? All of this, you see, deals with the question of personal and historical potentials, without an understanding of which psychoanalysis remains a retrospective, a "traumatological" psychology.

¶ Then you feel that the decision to use nonviolence was not necessarily a reflection of passivity at all, but rather represents an *active* inner process, the nature of which you want to determine. Is it possible that Gandhi was a brilliant master of strategy, and that nonviolence, rather than being merely a reflection of faith as many people saw it, reflected a definite strategy as well? In other words, is it possible that Gandhi's appearance of being simply a pious and austere man clouded our perception of his capabilities as an effective strategist?

Yes, very much so. In fact, Gandhi was never as pious and austere about himself as his followers and his translators make him appear. In studying the details of his personal life as they are reported to me now, I'm very much impressed to see what a marvelous sense of humor he had and how frankly conscious he was of being crafty and cunning as well as saintly, never seeing any contradiction between these qualities. It's often the purist followers or adversaries of a man like that who try to make a total saint, or total fraud, out of him. But Gandhi would just laugh and say, "Sure I'm a banya," which is the Indian equivalent for a crafty trader (like some connotations of "Yankee"), and he could afford to bargain and compromise, because he was quite clear about certain rock-bottom principles. It is both pleasant and important to describe that side of him, for it balances the often deeply neurotic implications of his inner conflicts and of his public contradictions.

¶ I imagine that as you began to examine in depth the sources, cultural context, application, and relative effectiveness of the so-called nonviolent techniques of social protest, you realized that you were dealing with an incredibly complex phenomenon, did you not?

Very much so. To illustrate this complexity, we should note that Gandhi was not only very much influenced by Thoreau, but also by Tolstoy and Ruskin. Furthermore, the success of civil disobedience and of nonviolence depends very much on the choice of time, place, and opponent. I will never forget the afternoon when one of my friends brought the African leader Mboya to my seminar at M.I.T., and the students asked him to discuss the prospective use of nonviolence by African nationalists. "Well," he said with a gracious smile and an elegant British accent, "I will tell you a simple rule. You can try it with the British but not with the Belgians." Nonviolence, he meant, presupposes a cultivated sense of fairness on the part of the opponent. The British officials, of course, could be very ruthless, but Gandhi was able to arouse interest and sympathy among the British of that period. He was British enough himself. He had studied in England, and had become an English barrister. He spoke and wrote English. Yet, I believe that there is something universal in his method. Incidentally, we prejudice the whole matter by calling it nonviolence or likening it to "passive resistance," which it isn't. Gandhi in many ways was one of the least passive persons you can imagine, and he carefully searched for a better name for nonviolence. He called it Satyagraha, which means "truth force." And he would be extremely active about it, you know, once he had chosen a time and a place. He would, for example, always announce in advance what he was going to do and when and where and he would move in on his opponents on schedule. The only passive thing about it was that he exacted a pledge from his people that they would not fight back if they were physically attacked, and not even swear back. But again, this demands (as some of our civil rights fighters know) a most active inner state as compared with the submissive, passive, and masochistic state which most Westerners would think it is. I am studying Gandhi's personal development and his exact technique in a given instant because I believe he may be both the last representative of a great trend in human history, and yet also the first in a new trend. In the past, religious man put himself in total opposition to political and technological man and strove for inner peace through noninvolvement, sacrifice, and faith. He often cultivated masochistic propensities; his ideal was saintliness. On the other hand, political and technological man has cultivated aggressive and expansive systems and has tried to build certain safeguards into them which would keep the peace in a limited area. By preparing for war against another area he tried to keep peace in his own. He has exploited the sadistic expression of man's rage, and given it a certain vaingloriousness. Needless to say, empires and churches have made territorial deals with each other, and deals which concerned what I like to call the territoriality of identity. Now, I think that Gandhi quite consciously established a new trend in combining politics and religion, and this at least temporarily with great psychological acumen. I do not know yet what I will come out with but I do feel that armament has developed to a point where man cannot indulge himself any further in technological vaingloriousness. The new situation challenges man's whole consciousness of his position in the universe on a grand new scale. And here Gandhi has a lasting message, beyond his moment in history, and beyond his ascetic philosophy.

Nonviolence and the American Civil Rights Movement

¶ Some of the specific patterns of civil rights protests in the United States seem to follow, at least superficially, along the same lines which characterized Gandhi's protest in India. For example, the time and place of a "lie-in" or "sit-in" are usually announced, and then the demonstration proceeds on schedule.

🐾 In terms of the example you mention, it is no accident that the method first had some success in our rural or small-town South. But the technology of communication has changed since Gandhi's day. Today the announcement of where and when a nonviolent approach will be used gets the press and the cameras there. What the ultimate effectiveness of civil disobedience might be where technology is so advanced will have to be seen.

¶ An example of what you allude to might be the reception given a group of demonstrators who announced they were going to use the nonviolent technique to protest an alleged discriminatory hiring policy of the New York World's Fair. As you may recall, they had their automobiles "run out of gas" on the opening day of the Fair, blocking its entrances. The cause advocated by the demonstrators was given no support by the communication media. In fact, the demonstration attempt aroused more hostility than support for the cause, and failed. Do you have any conceptions of possible causes of such failures in the use of nonviolent methods?

🐾 Gandhi always took an exceedingly simple and profound symbol out of which to make an issue. In 1930, he undertook to prove that even Indians have a right to take salt out of their own coastal waters without paying taxes to the British. He himself compared this laughingly with the Boston Tea Party. Tea and salt, you see. It has to be an issue of both symbolic and practical significance and it cannot be a local issue. You can choose a simply defined locality, such as a certain place on the Indian Ocean to test the salt tax, but salt itself is a universal issue. It is possible that the World's Fair issue was both too local and too sensational a setting.

¶ The example of a protest in support of desegregating a Southern college, then, would be a local test of an issue which has national implications?

That's right. That would be one college as a symbol for all colleges. But to try to interfere with the fun of a thing like the World's Fair, and this with a mechanical rather than human obstruction, may have missed the point.

3. Psychoanalysis and Its Impact: Philosophy, Theory, and Method

Psychoanalysis—Early Beginnings and Later Developments

¶ DR. EVANS: As an analyst and trainer of analysts, a researcher and observer, your work, as became evident as we discussed the eight stages of man, is rooted in Freudian theory. At this point we might discuss your feelings concerning Freudian theory and psychoanalysis, with respect to both specific constructs and their general philosophy. You do see yourself primarily as a psychoanalyst, do you not?

❦ PROFESSOR ERIKSON: Yes, I am primarily a psycho-analyst; it's the only method I have learned. And I feel lucky that as a clinician I started with child patients and young people under Anna Freud and August Aichhorn. Everything else I have done is an attempt to transfer a sense of dynamic development to fields bordering on the clinical. To do this, I have found it necessary to take long vacations from clinical practice. And I am learning a lot now from teaching a course on the life cycle to students who are very much in the middle of it. As to my first acquaintance with psychoanalysis, I don't know whether it would be called boasting or apologizing to say that I came to psychoanalysis from art. The majority of psychoanalysts in Vienna, as elsewhere, were physicians, but Sigmund Freud always felt that some people should enter psycho-analytic training from nonmedical fields. I think he always felt that psychoanalysis was something in between science and art, and while he had a genius for scientific clarity in obscure matters, he is unthinkable without the artistic element in his work. You may remember that his early case histories were said to read like novels, which can be a compliment but was than an opprobrium. His masterful analysis of Michelangelo's Moses, he published anonymously. It was his superb German style which first attracted me to his work, or rather, which early gave me a feeling that I "read him," even where I did not recognize all the theoretical implications.

¶ Freud's aesthetic interests become evident in several areas of his work, don't they?

❦ To me it is a continuous and intrinsic part of his work. But then, it was only one of its many facets.

¶ Were there quite a number of artists attracted to the psychoanalytic movement even as you were?

❦ Offhand, I do not know of any other artist who became a psychoanalyst, but there were several art historians. Ernst Kris was one of my teachers in the Vienna Institute while he was curator of the Vienna Art Museum, and Bruno Bettelheim, I believe, was an art historian.

¶ Very fascinating that you as an artist became familiar with Freud's work and could see the new horizons which it opened up. What happened after that?

❦ In those days candidates for psychoanalytic training were selected in quite another way than they are today. I think I was encouraged because as an artist I felt close to children. I was working under Peter Blos (who also became a psychoanalyst, and you undoubtedly know of his subsequent work on adolescence) in a small school in Vienna in which there were children undergoing child analysis. Anna Freud was at the time looking for people who might help her develop the psychoanalysis of children. So that is what I first specialized in, but the training, of course, included the psychoanalytic method as such.

¶ At that time it was rare for analysts to apply themselves particularly to the problems of children and work with them, was it not?

⚡ Definitely. In fact, when I came to Boston in 1933, I was the first psychoanalyst for children there. It was quite a new field then, but immediately recognized as important by some friends in the Harvard Medical School. This gave me my start, and I have been on medical school faculties ever since. I have to say, though, that many people find it too strenuous to practice child analysis after reaching middle age. I have often felt a bit delinquent in not pursuing it further, but was reassured the other day to hear that Anna Freud was not seeing children in private practice either.

Motivation beyond Libido Theory and Biological Determinism

¶ As we were able to discuss earlier, in your eight stages of man, you have done an intriguing job of paralleling Freud's biologically oriented developmental phases with a psychosocial developmental sequence, and you have tied in a pattern of virtues that develop along with the biological and psychosocial stages. Now, looking at this developmental model from a slightly different perspective, one is moved to ask the question concerning your views of motivation of the organism beyond the restrictions of libido theory: As you see it, by what units of energy beyond the "libido model" is he pulled forward in his development? Would you agree with at least some aspects of the motivational model posed by Freud's libido theory?

🐦 By now Freud's libido theory is rather an old theory, if you consider the progress of biological science since his time. And Freud himself once said, "The instincts are my mythology." In other words, he was clear about the fact that he was introducing a quantitative factor into emotional life which he suspected as being physiological in origin. But even in his own lifetime, Freud expected developments in glandular research and research in sexual biochemistry to replace his libido theory. After all, a theory is no more than the sum of the things to which it can give an initial order. But in the long run, it makes little sense, in view of scientific principles, to speak of energies which you cannot demonstrate. You may remember that Siegfried Bernfeld [5] did fundamental work on youth and ideology. He also once tried to create a "libidometric" method and to demonstrate that parts of the body vary in tonus and thus in libido. But you also know what happened to Wilhelm Reich, who took the libido theory too literally, as one often does with theories, and tried to reify (in the old sense of demonstrating a thing) a libidinal energy which he called "orgone" energy.

¶ He was the one who produced "orgone boxes," was he not?

❦ Yes; in fact, he got into a rather tragicomic conflict with the American Food and Drug laws because he was advertising and selling an energy which he couldn't demonstrate. I remember vividly how in 1933 I visited him on a Danish beach. He was camping and he told me that he saw the same bluish light which one sees around some stars passing between couples making love. Then I knew that the transition from nature philosophy to science had found a martyr in a once great clinical teacher.

¶ So you feel, then, that had Freud been living today he would reformulate his libido theory to conform to recent developments in the fields of biology, biochemistry, and physiology?

❦ I'm reasonably convinced of that.

¶ It was this particular construct which most disturbed Freud's dissenters, especially Adler and Jung, who felt that Freud's emphasis on the sexual motive was not borne out in their own clinical observations. Jung and Adler both saw power as the driving motive, and they included other types of motives that were fundamental to human behavior. What you intend to convey here, perhaps, is that it is irrelevant to argue these points any more. What is valid today has to reflect today's science.

❦ Well, recently Robert White [44] has spoken again of ego energies. He feels that the ego has an energy at its disposal which it uses in mastering the world, in developing competency. Very early in his career Freud tried to establish two instincts, the instinct of self-preservation and that of libido. This is rather reminiscent of nature philosophy which has been trying to divide the energy of organisms into two or three basic ones. Personally, I am not sympathetic to that, simply because this whole energetic viewpoint means rather little to me. There are, of course, many occasions—particularly in clinical practice —when Freud's libido theory seems to be the most suggestive way to classify what underlies observed behavior —but this is always symptomatic behavior in which an already aroused energy was suppressed and then found devious expression. In general, the configurational aspect is more congenial to me, that is, observable behavior in different contexts rather than energies which I cannot localize, which I cannot demonstrate, but which I nevertheless am supposed to name. I think my basic apprenticeship was watching children at play, and observing affects appear in changing contexts, and studying how fundamental human attitudes emerge and grow. New philosophical attitudes, I felt, could come only from that. The people of Freud's time were under the influence of the Victorian ethic, in which the child as well as the body in many ways was experienced as naughty, as a disturbance, as something you might enjoy surreptitiously but had to keep in abeyance or even suppress in order to attend to "higher" things. Freud had to show them that neither the child nor the body could be suppressed without grave consequences. In the meantime, world culture has changed in many respects, the body has come to be emancipated in many ways. At the same time, growth and development have become decisive in our work. Of course, the translation of Freud's term *Trieb* into "instinct" has perpetuated misunderstandings in the "biological" sphere.

¶ As I understand it, the old biological notion of the term "instinct" was that it was fixed and unchangeable. But by the word *Trieb* Freud really meant to suggest a modifiable drive.

⛏ I try to resolve this in my own work by differentiating between instinctive patterns and instinctual forces [14]. The instinctual forces in man are highly flexible and transferable drives, to which some such theory as the transformation of energy remains applicable. But man's drives are not nearly as much tied to a few instinctive behavior patterns as are the animal's.

¶ Continuing our discussion of Freudian motivation theory in a much broader vein, there seem to be shifts in emphasis going on which raise some basic questions for psychology. As we have been discussing, Freud's system suggested that man is especially shaped by physiological and biological forces; then the social determinists suggested that environmental factors were more important, going even to the extreme of some of the more radical views in that man is entirely shaped by his social environment. Lately, we seem to be returning to an older position that goes back through the entire history of philosophical and theological thought, and rediscovering the importance of self-responsibility. The question seems to be whether we are witnessing a normal pendulum-swing away from one extreme position toward another, or does this concern with self-responsibility, ego autonomy, and an existentialist posture represent a growing insecurity among men that they may be at the mercy of social and biological systems over which they have little control.

That is a very big question which touches on the overall ideological nature of social science. Since man, and especially suffering or conflicted man, always demands of any explanatory system a total answer, social scientists are apt to oblige and to totalize their methods. That aspect of man which you have learned to study, *is* man. If you have learned to study biological behavior, then you are apt to develop an ideological world view in which biological behavior (or whatever you can attach biological terms to) is the only relevant behavior. It would be better to maintain enough modesty to say that biological behavior is the only behavior which can be studied with biological methods. In regard to the social aspects of man, again a kind of totalistic simplification takes place in which it then looks as though man were only a social being. I would think the existentialist psychology is a reaction to all this. It claims that man's body and man's social environment are all part of his "phenomenological" world and the important thing really is how he experiences his own existence, and takes responsibility for it. But again, I would be interested in how man learns ontogenetically to experience his existence. Today I would be much more inclined to believe that every child very early has his own style of experiencing. But here the main point is that we are able to know and formulate such a small excerpt of our whole experience that it seems wrong to surrender our whole responsibility on earth (both metaphysical and very physical indeed) to any one system of knowledge.

¶ Your book *Insight and Responsibility* [12] also seems to bear on this question, does it not?

🐾 Yes, it does, in the sense that it deals with the application of therapeutic insights to different kinds of relationships. I spoke of "insight," rather than knowledge or fact, because it is so difficult to say in the study of human situations what you can really call knowledge. Whether in a therapeutic relationship, or in any other relationship outside the scientific laboratory, we can never claim that we ever act only on the basis of what we know—and yet act we always must. Insight guides us to what is worth studying, and it is also what emerges from our studies. If we put together everything we know, we still need insight for orientation and action. Then the question arises: how far can that insight guide us? This is of particular importance in a period when psychoanalysis, far from remaining an underground specialty, or being subjected to the nonconstructive interpretations which we just discussed, has become influential in education, literature, philosophy. And it may yet play a part in questions of war and peace. I feel that we have overdone the habit of thinking that our responsibility to the world is fulfilled by, or limited to, translating therapeutic insight into explanations of what went wrong and why in nonclinical contexts. The era of enlightenment, of which Freud was the last great representative, left us with the illusion that sufficient insight into pathology would lead man to be "better adjusted." This has even become part of a new political folklore. When I was there last, there was a medical convention in Delhi. One high dignitary of India who spoke at the opening told the physicians—or so the press reported—that the Chinese were obviously "insane," and that what we needed today was a cure for that kind of "insanity." To me, this represented a tragic misapplication of clinical theory. My wife and I happened to have a talk with him a few days after that meeting, and I tried politely to get him to tell me what he meant. He wisely refused to be pinned down. But the incident shows the extent to which faith in clinical enlightenment has spread to intelligent men of good will around the world.

¶ This brings to mind the distinction between intellectual insight and emotional insight. It's often thought that a simple articulation of meaning brings about changes in behavior, but this is not the case, and the therapist's responsibility goes beyond articulation of a superficial interpretation of behavior. The question then becomes: What is the "something else" for which the therapist is really responsible?

☞ Psychoanalysis is unique. It is *the* treatment situation in which intellectual insight is forced to become emotional insight under very carefully planned circumstances defined by technical rules. But outside of that situation, interpretations cannot do what they can do within a disciplined setting. For that we must study man in action and not just man reflecting on reality.

¶ Ordinarily, then, the natural settings within society are not conducive to insight beyond the intellectual level, and therefore not capable of bringing about behavioral change.

☞ I point out in my book [12] that we have learned more about how man views the world in terms of "reality" than we have learned about his relationship to *actuality*. It makes sense to me to differentiate between reality and actuality. Both terms go back to the German word *Wirklichkeit*, which Freud used originally. But *Wirklichkeit* has to do with *wirken*, which means to act in order to effect. The world becomes real to you not only because you recognize it as existing but also because you "realize" it in action. What we have learned in all these decades about child development is not just how a child learns to recognize and to appreciate reality, but also by what measures and in what situations he will feel activated to use his best potential and to activate others likewise. It isn't enough, then, to show people the reality of certain existing facts or underlying forces. We must also show them how man can activate man and be activated by him in such a way that the binding forces of Eros become operative. Psychoanalysis has revealed the irrational thinking which hinders reality testing, but has not given its due to actuality. This bridge is as yet to be built.

¶ You're implying that the impact on society of the psychoanalytic model has led it to its first step, interpretation, but the real important step then, the mechanism for activation, has not been provided, that perhaps psychoanalysis should lend itself more to be used as a tool for exploring problems of broader scope than the clinical setting. Didn't Freud, in some of his later writings, also suggest such expansion?

One must always emphasize that Freud as a doctor, a citizen, a writer, and a philosopher, always transcended his own theories. In many ways, Freud was a much more inclusive person than a cursory knowledge of some of his writings would indicate. Someone said to him once, "You analyze immorality, but you say little about morality." He answered, "Morality I take for granted." One can't emphasize enough how many things Freud took for granted —all the values, facts, and conditions of the pre–World War I bourgeoisie *within* which he wanted to bring about change. To us, all of these have now become dated circumstances made fluid by progress as well as war and revolution. That is why the question of identity could not conceivably be central in his thinking.

¶ So what we are saying here is that since Freud's time we have seen shifts in our patterns of thinking and understanding human personality.

🖗 The question is complicated by the fact—as we discussed briefly earlier—that it's not just a matter of different ways of thinking but also of different historical periods. Freud belonged to a period of history which came to an end with his generation. He worked as an erstwhile physiologist in a setting in which the stability and cultural dominance of the upper middle class in Europe was taken for granted. It was not quite as possible to see the social and cultural relativity of psychological phenomena in his time. Since then, of course, revolutions of all kinds have become universal and wars have become global. Freud and almost all of his followers had to emigrate from the European continent.

¶ You're saying that a contributor to any area of knowledge, no matter how brilliant or perceptive he may be, is still to some degree a man of his times.

❦ I would certainly say so, even if he transcends his times and helps to create a new era.

Psychoanalysis as a Technique of Psychotherapy

¶ Addressing ourselves now more specifically to psychoanalysis as a technique of therapy, one of the questions which is being raised today concerns the value of psychoanalysis over less intensive methods of treatment. I wonder how you as a psychoanalyst and trainer of psychoanalysts might feel about this.

❦ It is always unwise (as well as unprofessional) for any psychotherapeutic persuasion to claim that it could cure the people that others could not cure. In fact, I believe that psychoanalysis is the preferred method for fewer types of patients than are now undergoing psychoanalysis. In many urban areas it has become a fad as well as a replacement for lost rituals, such as an ideology or religion may provide. This, too, may have its uses, and I think that today experts must take over in many areas previously covered by religious dogma. But it is important to know what one is being used for. And psychoanalysis does deal "expertly" and specifically with such matters as guilt which were and in some ways are the true domain of religion. But to come back to therapy itself. When I first began to practice in this country and reported my early cases to Anna Freud in Vienna, she wrote back to me that some of the cases I described would never have been accepted for psychoanalytic treatment in Vienna. I feel we must acknowledge that we may not be able to separate at any given time what gives a method general appeal, what makes it good for the patient, and what makes it especially congenial for the psychotherapist. It is not enough for the psychotherapist to claim that he has learned his method only because he knew it would work better than any other (reasonably honest) method. The fact is, he can really learn only a method which is compatible with his own identity. Compatibility with his own identity is a minimum condition for his effectiveness with patients to whom his method has appeal. It is no coincidence that all over the world a large percentage of the first psychoanalysts and probably also of patients were Jewish. I think Freud believed himself, that in some ways the whole logic of psychoanalysis has much to do with highly verbal and self-conscious gifts, and we know to what extent book learning and verbal drive have been an important part of Jewish identity and adaptation over the centuries. So it isn't just a question of which method is the best for patients, but also of which method the therapist feels most at home with and creative in. Only then will he be a really good therapist for the patients whom he has learned he is good for. Yet all of this does not preclude the wider application of a method, once it has found its theoretical bearings. While psychoanalysis may not be the preferred method in all cases, it may be a method applicable to much more than therapy. It may be the principal modern form of systematic introspection and meditation. I think Erich Fromm [21] has pursued this in writing about the relationship of psychoanalysis and Zen. In *Young Man Luther* [8], which we discussed earlier, I have indicated the possibility that there is an historical continuity in the Judaeo-Christian mind between soul-searching prayer and self-analysis. So it is not all a matter of being cured of isolated symptoms (that kind of cure one may sometimes buy more cheaply), but of learning to become aware of your elemental conflicts. So if psychoanalysis is a method of staying in touch with man's inner resources and with his unavoidable conflicts, its derivatives may have a supreme function in the technological world of the future. Psychoanalysis is the first systematic and active "consciousness-expansion," and such expansion may be necessary as man concentrates on the conquest of matter and is apt to over-identify with it.

¶ Isn't it true that in Freud's later life he began to become less enchanted with psychoanalysis as a treatment technique?

Yes. Freud was always quite frank in saying that his first motivation was curiosity and not the wish to cure. This may sound a little cold-blooded, but he meant it as a useful warning that many people by an exaggerated wish to cure, may do more harm than good.

¶ In view of this assessment of psychoanalysis, what different orientations would you suggest?

To answer your question, I would first have to say that psychoanalysis has necessarily emphasized a retrospective view, and that its interpretations are based on reconstruction. I certainly would not want to abandon continuing research in this. I wouldn't want to become a pre-Freudian in this respect either. On the contrary, I feel that a psycho-historical way of understanding the collective past, as we discussed earlier, will grow out of the method of the case history. And the life-history approach, the study of lives-in-progress, as R. W. White calls it,* will teach us more about our cases, that is, about the conditions for regression. But I would think that in a post-Freudian development the therapist would always be aware of the fact that he is taking a planful place in an ongoing life and that every acute life crisis also arouses new energies in the patient. We all know this but we do not always act on what we know, and we are not always aware of the fact that our interpretive habits are social action. Reconstruction presupposes patients strong enough to learn by introspective insight. So even the most passive therapeutic attitude is action, even if it leads temporarily to a deliberate choice of no action. In the scientific laboratory it is permissible to say, "I can't make the next move because I don't know enough yet," and go home and hope for a better day. But in the human labora-

* For a detailed discussion of this approach, see R. W. White, *Lives in Progress* (New York: Dryden Press, 1952). The use of case histories as a pedagogical device contributing to understanding or study of personality, has also been used by a number of other authors, e.g. G. W. Allport [2] and D. C. McClelland [33].

tory you commit yourself to a future by whatever you say or do not say. And then, to publish and to publicly defend your interpretive habits is social action on a large scale. As I mentioned earlier, there was a time when psychoanalysis could consider itself an underground movement shared only by those who could afford Freud's collected papers in a luxurious leather edition. Today, Freud and others are available in paperback, and descriptions of psychoanalytic "technique" are accepted as prescriptions for adjustment. One must realize that psychoanalysis has gained new insights in the process of treating new classes of patients and of understanding shifts in the epidemiology of neuroses. Early psychoanalytic work, it seems, was restricted primarily to certain kinds of morally rather well-integrated and verbally very gifted individuals who were inhibited and repressed, or split in their personalities, and whose symptoms kept them from using their potentials in ways they knew they wanted to use them. So the analyst tried to restore their free will to his patients. Since Freud's time, however, we have learned to deal with many more kinds of patients.

¶ As suggested by your earlier point concerning the fact that everyone has access to these psychoanalytic ideas, haven't many psychoanalytic notions been inadequately applied?

℣ As in all fields close to medicine there are two questions: when is a man demonstrably sick, and when is he really healthy, that is, more than not-sick, in the sense of a medical chart full of "negs." What we have discussed today is in a certain liveliness and spirited quality which is more than a mere absence of severe conflict. But then in a culture with over-defined mental diseases there is also the danger of a patient's acquiring what I call a patient identity. In a world eager to diagnose and type, it can happen that a young patient whose disturbance is part of an identity crisis, becomes almost too eager to be diagnosed. He assumes the role which the diagnosis seems to suggest to him. Patients of this sort feel at times more integrated as patients than they ever did as non-patients. My son, Kai Erikson—a sociologist—has written about that [15].

¶ The patient then becomes almost too comfortable in a "deviant" role. This gets at the whole problem that the community psychiatry movement is attempting to counteract. The argument is that when the patient is hospitalized he receives so much attention from the staff and becomes so comfortable that he doesn't want to leave. He becomes too well adjusted to a hospital setting.

❦ Yes, that is one aspect of what I mean.

¶ Regarding now the notion of mental health as a "movement," it would be quite difficult for a psychoanalyst, psychiatrist, or psychologist (as you intimate) were he challenged to really adequately define the concept, so that formulas *guaranteed* to insure "good mental health" can be communicated to society. Yet our pressing concern with mental health may have forced us to allow our perhaps premature speculations on this matter to seep into popular culture. Can this not lead to considerable misinterpretation of various types of behavior and contribute in an unconstructive manner to an overconcern with this problem?

To read pathography always means to find some of the symptoms described in oneself or in one's children. And biographers tell us that some of the most creative people also had unusually severe symptoms. So the central question is whether a person has a neurosis or the neurosis has him. But to deplore the excess interpretations which are now becoming too easy and too habitual, does not mean to reverse ourselves and to seek a pre-Freudian innocence. The point is to keep the insights we have gained in regard to man's instinctual dangers and yet also learn from the fate of these insights in the post-Freudian era. When retrospective therapeutic analyses become popular reading matter, then our restorative responsibility expands. And that is why I emphasize prospective aspects of the life cycle. If we can continue to think of the child or youth as a growing person, then we avoid seeing his disturbed behavior only as a result of a traumatic past, and learn to appraise it as a block in his present development. A truly enlightened mother of today would have reasonable confidence in her own judgment of where her child is going or wants to go. She would not say, "You are destructive and I know why," least of all in a scolding tone which would equate the "reason" with weakness or badness, but she would spontaneously lead him toward new activities ready in him. But, of course, there are children too blocked to be ready for anything new and they (and/or their mothers) need treatment.

¶ To look at this in a broader sense, psychoanalysis has an impact on a wide variety of social institutions. As we briefly mentioned earlier, Freud—for instance—postulated an ultimate mature, creative, unselfish level of development which he described as the genital level. This notion has been expanded and enlarged upon by Erich Fromm [e.g. 17] into the productive orientation, and is dealt with in *The Art of Loving* [22]. Both of these character types are more or less related to the ethical system of the society and the golden rule. However, it is not easy to define the golden rule in a psychological, operational sense.

Maybe somewhat brashly, I invented a version of the golden rule when I had to explain to medical students how our present-day knowledge of development may affect ethics [11, 12]. The golden rule in its traditional form—that is, "do (or do not) unto another what you wish him to do (or not to do) unto you"—has, of course, as you have suggested, been criticized as illogical and impossible to fulfill. George Bernard Shaw, facetiously as always, warned us not to abide by it because, he said, your tastes and the other's tastes may differ, so how do we know what another wants or does not want to be done by? But then, after all, principles aren't here to be fulfilled but to serve as guidelines. I would amend the golden rule by starting with the assumption that it makes little sense to tell a mother and a child, or a man and a woman, or a doctor and a patient, to abide by the golden rule in the treatment of each other, because they are in mutual and reciprocal relationships of inequality and have different needs as a result of differing in sex, age, or station in life. Now that we are increasingly enlightened in regard to the different needs of different people at different stages of life, maybe we should learn to do to another what helps him to fulfill his potentials even as it helps us to fulfill ours. This, you may note, is really the principle of mutuality in genitality. It is also a principle which we have learned in psychotherapy, but it should be applicable to other unequal relationships, such as that of parent and child. This is love, but it is not always "loving" in expression. It can call for ruthless indignation, and it may hurt. But a principle, after all, only guides us in thinking over situations in which we have failed to do spontaneously what we must then learn to do planfully. To many, no doubt, it "comes naturally." Does that make any sense to you?

¶ Yes. You're really talking about a mutual shaping effect.

🐾 Yes, mutuality, in fact, is the key word.

¶ When we speak of shaping effects, we are confronted by the existentialists, who wonder just who is to do the shaping. As in fact we discussed earlier, is the person himself going to be given the responsibility for the direction of growth, or should it be imposed from the outside? When we deal with parents and psychotherapists, this becomes a fine line of distinction.

🐾 Very fine. Yes. The therapeutic encounter, as it is often called today, implies that the therapist has a strong sense of where the patient is going—potentially. As long as the therapist tries to impose his own future or his own past on the patient's development, he is not maturing as a psychotherapist or as a person. This is implicit in the whole notion of transference and countertransference, which tells the therapist that he must not respond to the patient's infantile demands with his own infantile needs and wishes. And yet on the other hand, we know that we cannot avoid doing just that to some extent. But if we understand it in time we respond to a challenge and also make an important step toward helping the patient become what he can become. I believe in your dialogue with Jung [16] he said, "Every patient who comes to me takes his life in his own hands." This is true, but one must add that he came to *me*, and not to somebody else, and after that he will never be the same—and neither will I. This is why we insist that any therapist should (by temperament, education, and self-analysis) be prepared to identify with a variety of alternative life plans, so that he will not force any patient into too narrow a mold. It is unfortunate that such prescriptions always sound moralistic, while they are simply part of therapeutic actuality.

¶ In terms of your more specific conceptions of the therapeutic relationship, should the attempt to avoid countertransference mean that the therapist should play as impersonal a role as possible?

Had you known Freud in his older age or Anna Freud and her generation in Vienna, you could not assume that the rule of impersonality could mean anything but a relative guideline for an impartial acceptance of a willing patient's free associations, and of his pre-analytic past. This does not suggest forgetting one's own values or making oneself a piece of adjunct equipment to the couch. The important thing is not that the therapist make himself impersonal, but that he realize what particular kind of countertransferences he is apt to develop out of habitual irrational inclinations, and that he will not let these interfere. The therapist as a person is always there, and any interpretation he gives cannot avoid expressing what he feels or thinks passionately about.

¶ Are you implying, then, that the model for psychotherapy would incorporate all the ingredients of any mature human relationship?

🐦 Yes, insofar as it is clear who is "the doctor" and who is the patient, and that their respective functions determine what the next step in maturity would be for each. I would apply the golden rule only where the actual function of both partners is clearly seen. In fact, I don't think it is necessary to insist that the therapist should be neutral or paternal, or loving, or human, or anything else, because I would think that all relationships in human life are defined by the mutuality of function, and so is the therapeutic one. It needs no ennobling by "as if" pretensions. The psychoanalytic situation is merely a model of "competent" behavior considering the subject matter it must deal with. And what is true for the therapist, is true for all other relationships: mutuality, competence, and the development of capacities go together. Love includes them all. To be a good therapist ought to be good enough for anyone.

Psychoanalysis and Broad Ethical Considerations

¶ Our discussion of psychoanalysis has implicitly touched frequently on the matter of ethics. Do you feel it is possible for a psychologist to maintain his identity as an investigator when he becomes involved in the analysis of problems involving moral and ethical dimensions, or is he more likely to fall into the trap of totalizing his methods, as you mentioned before?

🐦 Maybe the totalization is a symptom of the denial of the fact that dealings with human beings always include ethical involvement. In this respect, I find I must take issue with some scientific pretensions in my own field. Freud, of course, did create a psychology with physiological and naturalistic concepts. And Hartmann, you may have noticed, reaffirmed Freud's position in his book on *Psychoanalysis and Moral Values* [24], in which he ascribes to ethics the place of a mere subject matter for psychoanalysis and deplores the false uses of psychoanalysis as a support of contemporary values. Of course, he is quite right when he says that psychoanalysis has to be prepared to consider moral values as relative, since it must give impartial attention to members of many different religions, countries, races and periods. This is especially important since moralisms and extreme moral attitudes help to make man neurotic. This very insight, in fact, marks the place of psychoanalysis in social evolution.

¶ What you're saying, then, is that the very moral structure is a contributing factor in mental health, and therefore is a legitimate area for concern, but that should not be confused with the over-all problem of ethics.

Ⓥ That's right. If you mean man's inner moral structure, it does predispose him to moralism, to cruel moral dogmatism, and to prejudice against others and against himself. But I think it would help to differentiate man's moral sense and his ethical sense developmentally. This insight has been delayed by our exclusive concern with childhood (a reaction to the previous neglect), and by our now taking adulthood for granted.

¶ A good illustration of this might be Freud's construct of superego, where he is trying to illustrate dynamically how the whole impact can lead to some dissociation in the individual. Then the legitimate concern for psychoanalysis is the dissociation, but it is still not exactly the same thing as looking objectively at ethics.

☙ It is, insofar as the moral sense is basic to the ethical one. So we would not want to make the superego appear to be expendable. It is an essential part of man's inner structure. Where we run into difficulties is in the ideological use of this concept in our time. Freud's criticism of Victorian morals has today been turned into an antimoralistic ideology. Some young people look to Freud as a champion of complete relativism in moral matters, which was quite alien to him.

¶ There was a similar consequence when Freudian theory opened the door for the acceptance and exchange of love with a child. Many people misinterpreted this to mean that the child should be allowed complete freedom with no restrictions whatsoever. We often see this kind of reaction to a position where the opposite extreme is picked up.

☙ This leads us back to a differentiation between morals and ethics. If conduct is only a matter of either being moralistic or being antimoralistic, then we are led only to a misuse of psychoanalytic insight. You see, we have here another consequence of the fact that psychoanalysis has so largely formulated matters in infantile terms. The superego, where it is dominant, can only reinforce moralistic or, if you permit, moralistically antimoralistic attitudes. Luckily, however, an ideological sense is acquired in adolescence, and an ethical one in young adulthood. And many of our most sincerely rebellious youths are really looking for a new ethical system in which it would be unnecessary to be either moralistic or antimoralistic. I believe that a wider human identity paired with universal communication and science may well accomplish this— not as a utopia, but as a necessity. Because man could well blow himself up with moralistic and ideological conviction.

Conclusion: Man's Survival in a Nuclear Age

¶ Professor Erikson, we've covered several hopefully provocative and timely subjects here, and learned a great deal about your feelings on a number of subjects. Perhaps we could look to the future here a moment and explore your reactions to the fact that technological development has moved to a point where we can really destroy ourselves quite easily. And yet the knowledge and understanding in human relations is very minute in comparison. We seem to have developed techniques for destroying all of mankind without having developed truly effective means by which men can communicate with and understand each other. If you were to make a prediction, do you think that this will eventually lead to man's destruction or do you feel that he can bridge this gap?

🪶 After some very traumatic moments I think we are closer to the Russians now, and the Russians to us in recognizing that we are dependent on each other. I know little about this, but I've heard scientists discuss the whole matter and they seem to be more hopeful at the moment that this whole apocalyptic machinery could have built-in brakes which might prevent a nuclear war. But this is like putting the brake before the engine. After all, "the bomb" is only one item in a whole enormous development of techniques by which man may destroy and harm himself. He may not only blow himself up with an atom bomb, but he may, as we have read recently in Rachel Carson's [7] book, poison his woods and his water at home now, and outer space in the future. He may also create a way of life for himself which personality and organism cannot bear or (even if specialized organisms and personalities survive) which the generational process cannot bear. The utopia of today it seems to me is based on a reduction in the number of births *and* a new ethic based on a greater awareness of what each generation owes to the next. It is not just a matter for survival, for man can "survive" under conditions no animal could stand. It is a matter of using man's constructive capacities, so latent rage will not be fed by their misuse. All over the world today there is more of a sense of what we owe to the underprivileged at home and abroad, and a "more inclusive" sense that whatever is going to happen to the next generation in any country is our problem today. Here again, as I said before, I feel women have a great role to play, but women should make it more clear to themselves what kind of world they feel their children can live in, and should translate it all into political demands. They also need to take part in governmental, scientific, and legislative pursuits which affect the lives of the generations. And maybe if women come to terms with their "masculinity," men will accept their own "femininity" and, for example, stop considering peacefulness unmanly.

¶ You're suggesting that we perhaps have already in operation a mechanism which can span this gap in technological versus social development? Perhaps the increasing concern for the development of human potential will be the brake which will ward off total destruction and perhaps lead us to make more progress in human relations.

Yes, there seems to be such a spontaneous, almost revolutionary development.

¶ I can't tell you how much we appreciate your kindness in participating in our project, and your patience and skill exhibited in answering my many questions. Thank you very much. Is there anything you would like to add?

❧ You have heard of the rabbi who felt inhibited when he was asked to make a speech in heaven. "I am good only at refutation," he said. My difficulty is different. I find it hard to put up a good argument, because I am more at home in observation and illustration. But you have been a good guide through difficult terrain.

Conclusion:
The Theoretical Context
of the Dialogue

Rather than attempt to ferret out systematically all of the major concepts presented in the dialogue, as in the previous volumes based on Jung and Fromm, I shall again take the liberty briefly to present frameworks which I find valuable in teaching personality theory to students, hoping they may in turn be of value to the reader in comprehending the backdrop against which we may look at contemporary contributors to the understanding of personality, such as Erik H. Erikson. As I indicated in the first section, Freudian theory was used as one focal point of comparison in the questions programmed for Erikson. However, other perspectives also provided some of the rationale for the questions utilized in the discussion. These are three frameworks around which I believe current approaches to personality can be analyzed in order to help to locate any theoretical position within the matrix of general personality theory. They are really descriptive approaches to the understanding of personality which develop theoretically from basic orientations focusing around biological determinism, cultural determinism, or self-determinism.

One group of contributors, apparently emphasizing biological determinism, has been considered more or less traditionally psychoanalytical. It includes such writers as Hans Sachs and Ernest Jones, as well as Freud himself. This group has been characterized as emphasizing what Freud called "repetition compulsion," a concept which maintains that the first five years of life, which are strongly influenced by biological propensities, are very important in human development because they set the stage for and determine a life style which is manifested continuously throughout the individual's lifetime; central to this postulate is the notion of the Oedipal complex. Another important aspect of traditional Freudian theory was brought out by Ernest Jones in our earlier published dialogue with him [16], in which he unabashedly makes the statement, "Well, man is, after all, an animal." Some people think that this is a cynical view, although Jones denied that Freud was inordinately cynical. Freud's earliest picture of man is that of an organism dominated to a large degree by its id—the animal, biological side of him —against which the ego—the conscious, the self of man— is fighting a tough battle. He is seen as just barely able to hold his head above water in the struggle to keep from being drowned by the animal he basically is. This view of man, as articulated in Freud's early works, was also accepted by many of the early followers of Freud. With Freud, they believed that the center of man's motivation and energy is the sexual libido, which to them was a manifestation of the dominant animal aspect of man. Although Freud in his later work began to emphasize other aspects of man's make-up also, many thinkers continue to perceive the classical psychoanalytical position in terms of these early views of Freud. Actually, the above description is probably a vast oversimplification of Freud's view, as Fromm, for example, implied in our earlier volume [17].

Another group of contributors, the neo-Freudians, has placed more stress on the effects of cultural influences on man's development. To the neo-Freudians, the early Freudians would appear to have taken too seriously the notion that the instinctual animal nature, the repetition compulsion, and a general biological patterning of early development is found *universally,* and that these elements dominate man's nature. The neo-Freudians take exception to this concept of universality. They believe that man is primarily a product of the specific kind of culture in which he lives, and that learning plays a much more important part than does biological patterning in the development of personality.

The late Karen Horney, for example, a prominent neo-Freudian who had been with the Berlin Psychoanalytic Institute, became so disturbed by many notions in the biological orientation of the early Freudian position, such as the postulation of male superiority (evidenced by the assertion that penis envy was characteristic of women), that she broke away from the orthodox Freudian position. She developed a view [e.g. 26] that man is shaped to a significant extent by the society with which he must cope when he deals with the anxieties of reality. She considered this anxiety produced by societal pressures more important in shaping man than his anxiety about overcoming his basic biological animal nature.

Again, as indicated in our earlier volume [17], although Fromm does not like the label neo-Freudian, he too certainly takes exception to Freud's emphasis on the Oedipal situation so central to Freud's "biological unfolding" view of man's development.

Other psychologists have attempted to place man within his social milieu, in the belief that it constitutes the essential force in shaping personality. In spite of the fact that Freud later appeared to be placing more emphasis on the importance of society as a formative influence in the development of individual personality, traditional Freudian theory as it is most often expounded does not emphasize this element. The neo-Freudians made dominant this aspect of man's relationship to his world, emphasizing a cultural determinism which constitutes a departure from what is customarily regarded as traditional Freudian theory. Had Freud emphasized this aspect of the relationship earlier in his writings, he might not have acquired the reputation for being so biologically oriented. At any rate, many of his immediate followers certainly perpetuated a biological orientation, whereas the neo-Freudians, represented by Horney [e.g. 26], Abram Kardiner [e.g. 29], and Harry Stack Sullivan [e.g. 41], deviated from that point of view. The neo-Freudian group challenged psychoanalysis to extend the study of man at least beyond Freud's early basic tenets.

Another characteristic of the neo-Freudian group is evident in their techniques of psychotherapy. The older Freudians considered psychotherapy a five-day-a-week affair which takes from three to five years of intensive therapy before it can be successful; the neo-Freudians, utilizing recent innovations, believe that situational factors are much more important, and claim to have achieved results with much shorter periods of psychotherapy.

Somewhere between the neo-Freudians and the traditional Freudians there is a group of three significant individuals whom we might describe as Freudian dissentients; for although each of them worked closely with Freud, each subsequently broke with him or was repudiated by him for one reason or another. Carl Jung, Otto Rank, and Alfred Adler constitute this group.

By all accounts, Adler's early work placed the primary

emphasis on the social man, and it might be said that Adler set the stage for the emergence of the neo-Freudian group. In a different direction, although many of his ideas about early biological conceptions were in agreement with Freud's, Rank's preoccupation with the "will" [e.g. 36] and its development of autonomy introduced a type of self-determinism that Freud apparently did not emphasize.

As became apparent in our dialogue with Carl Jung [16], he had moved away from Freud's basic tenets, while retaining Freud's idea of the unconscious, expanding it into a race and individual unconscious and incorporating into the race unconscious Freud's early notion of archetypes, developing this concept beyond Freud's postulation. However, with his central conception of individuation Jung also moved away from the emphasis on biological determinism. Jung, perhaps more profoundly than either Adler or Rank, turned toward the idea of the development of an ultimately self-determined spiritual being which transcends the biological forces acting on man. This led him to consider many metaphysical conceptions, obviously not in keeping with present-day notions of a scientific psychology.

A great deal of thought today continues to reflect the greater concern for man's individuality and self-responsibility than is found in either biological or cultural determinism. For example, the position of the existentialists—particularly in the works of Rollo May [32], the distinguished philosophical theologian Paul Tillich [42], the philosophers Husserl [27] and Heidegger [25], and the work of Carl Rogers [37] in the United States—reflects this concern, as does the work of Abraham Maslow [31] in recent years. Obviously many other psychologists have currently reflected an increased concern with the autonomy of the self, for example Allport [1] and McCurdy [34].

However, it must be kept in mind that related to any theoretical discussion of "determinism" and personality theory, the behavioristic orientation is still perhaps the most significant theoretical referent for psychologists. Contemporary views (such as for example those of Skinner [40], Wolpe [45], and Bandura [4], interpret not merely cultural influences in a broad sense, but environmental determinism in a narrow sense as being the significant shaping force on the individual. As they control environment experimentally and even in the clinical situation, they make very few assumptions concerning the "internal workings" of personality.

Questions in the dialogue were designed to obtain reactions from Erik Erikson concerning the three orientations described above, but did not particularly relate his views to a strictly behavioristic orientation, since it is obvious that this would have involved a different level of analysis in this context, since Erikson clearly operates out of a different set of assumptions.

At various points in the dialogue Professor Erikson was given an opportunity to deal directly or indirectly with the differences among the three positions represented by the biological, the cultural, and the self-deterministic points of view. I believe we can say that in his eight stages of man, he has integrated all of these three conceptualizations into a unique system which is very broad in perspective. His concern with the psychosocial development and its attendent emphasis on the development of "values" and "virtues" as parallel developments with the biological growth and development, appears to be a provocative and profound extension of Freud's work. Tied in with the work of Piaget [e.g. 35] and others, this would appear to present many hypotheses for significant research.

Only within recent years has social science come to recognize the need to involve itself with issues of immediate concern to society. This science, like many in more strictly experimentally oriented areas, has been inclined to develop for what might appear to the outsider to be the exclusive benefit of members of its diverse but interrelated disciplines. On the current scene Erikson has been in the forefront of this broadening of the viewpoint of the social sciences. As some recent discussions have emphasized (e.g. Sanford [39], Evans [18]), a case can be made for a greater concern for human problems within the province of psychology. The unique creative efforts of Erikson appear to provide provocative base lines for such endeavors.

In conclusion, it must be said that aside from anything else he does, Erik H. Erikson is one of the truly creative contributors not only to psychology, psychiatry, and psychoanalysis, but undoubtedly to an understanding of the human predicament in the broadest sense.

REACTIONS FROM
ERNEST JONES

The interview with Dr. Jones which follows provides an opportunity for unique contrast between Erikson and Jones, both in connection with their own ideas and in connection with their respective opinions concerning many of Freud's theoretical formulations. Dr. Jones devoted much of his life to supporting the views of Sigmund Freud, and his last major contribution, a three-volume biography of Freud, represents a massive tribute to Freud the man as well as Freud the scholar.

As Dr. Jones' responses will indicate, throughout the interview he was sharp, satirical, and bound and determined to defend Freud against his critics to the end. The reader will note, however, that even when Dr. Jones responded in a satirical or very forceful manner, he never lost his pedantic, proper British sense of proportion.

Reactions from Ernest Jones

Dr. Evans: Dr. Jones, one of the questions that I believe has been of very great interest to many of our students of psychology in America centers around your own relationship to the psychoanalytic movement. Of course, you have discussed this in other places, but hearing from you something about how you happened to become involved with the psychoanalytic movement will be very interesting.

Dr. Jones: Well, I find that an interesting question too, because I was the first person outside of Vienna and Zurich to do so. Why was I? Well, I suppose you could go back to infantile impressions and stimulations, which would take us a long way away, but historically speaking, it comes to this: In my teens I was very interested in general spiritual problems of religion, of sociology, of socialism, of philosophy; and it occurred to me that the most fundamental way to get at the basis for all these problems would be to study the nervous system, the brain, in which case, of course, I was obviously woefully mistaken. So I became a neurologist and I did quite a bit of work in neurology, original work, some of which is still extant; and naturally came across patients with what we nowadays call neurotic symptoms. That's what happens to every neurologist. He thinks he is studying something organic, and he comes across these other cases; they come to him.

So my interest swerved from that, from the organic side, to the other; and I began reading and learning everything I could. I read the whole French literature on that, on multiple personality, or split-off sections of it. There was Janet; there were Breuer and Binet; and there were different French writers for about a hundred years, especially in the use of hypnosis. Well, as far as that goes, I used hypnosis myself, trying to explore and find out more about what was going on behind the scenes. It became evident to me that when you've got a simple hysterical symptom, there was something much more complicated behind it that was not visible. I wanted to get at that.

Dr. Evans: This was then not too long after Freud's *Interpretation of Dreams* (10) had been . . .

Dr. Jones: . . . had been published. It wasn't the first thing I heard of Freud, however. I knew about his organic neurological work through my neurological studies. He'd published even in English periodicals—in *Brain*, a British journal called *Brain*.

Dr. Evans: So his neurological work, on its own, already had gotten quite a lot of attention, even before he got into his . . .

Dr. Jones: Oh, very much so. I mean he was one of the leading neurologists in Europe. Even to this day his work on paralyses in childhood are the classic books on the subject, as is his work on aphasia and other things. He was well known in England at that time as a leading neurologist.

Then I heard of his doing this other work, and he described a case which he called the "daughter analysis." It was at the beginning of 1905, and I was very impressed by that. I thought it so astonishing that there was a man who seemed to listen to his patients—listen to what they said. I had never heard of anybody doing that, and that was really the feature about his work that struck me most. So I thought I would start listening to my patients more in detail than I had before.

Dr. Evans: Then at first you heard of this man as a colleague in neurology and became interested in this other phase of his work. Apparently you had noticed these psychological factors in your own patients, but here was a man who probed more deeply into them. After that you went to Vienna, I understand.

Dr. Jones: Three years later. I was studying abroad in Munich and Paris before that, both neurology and psychiatry, under Kraepelin in Munich. I worked under him for months.

Dr. Evans: On first meeting Dr. Freud, did you find that your hope that this would unfold new avenues and new sources of understanding was realized rather rapidly? In other words, from your early discussions with Dr. Freud, were you rather well convinced that this would be something perhaps of life-long interest to you?

Dr. Jones: Oh, I think even before I met him—yes. I met Dr. Jung before then and at a time when he was very enthusiastic about Freud's work; and we were both enthusiastic about it together. It was he who introduced me to Freud, I mean personally. That meeting took place at the First Analytical Congress, at Salzburg, in April, 1908. We met there, and Dr. Jung introduced me to Freud.

Dr. Evans: At this time was Dr. Adler already part of this group?

Dr. Jones: Oh yes, he was. He and Stekel were the two first, I reckon, who followed Freud at all. They date back to 1902.

Dr. Evans: To go further into your own feelings about Dr. Freud's work and your relationship with Dr. Freud, as we look at psychology, psychoanalysis, and psychiatry today, we are struck by the fact that Dr. Freud's contribution seems to postulate a strong biological pattern which he suggests has a tremendous effect on the early development of the individual. These biological patterns, though they are modifiable by the environment or the culture within which the individual lives, nevertheless continue to direct the individual to great extent.

Very recently, as you know, there have been a number of people who feel that perhaps Dr. Freud and the psychoanalysis of this period emphasized biological factors a bit too much, that maybe the culture in which we live, our society and environmental surroundings, have as much or more effect in the molding of the individual than do these biological factors. I wonder if you would like to comment on this in terms of whether, first of all, we are unfair in suggesting that Freud was over-emphasizing biological factors; and secondly, about those views emphasizing cultural factors, that stem from the so-called "neo-Freudian" movement. How would Freud have reacted to them?

Dr. Jones: No, I don't think for a minute it would be fair to say that he was over-emphasizing the importance of biological factors. I don't see how anybody could over-estimate them. Freud took the view, and I take the view too, that man is an animal. In other words, man is in line biologically with the rest of living creatures and is actuated by instincts and reactions of a similar kind, though certainly of a more elaborate kind. That is in the nature of things, the basis of man's being. You can take another view and say that that is only part of his being, and that there is the spiritual part which came from the sky and was put into him on top of it all; but we don't happen to take that view. There doesn't seem to be any direct evidence for it. I don't see how you can over-estimate the nature of man.

When you come to cultural influences, they too are the produce of the biological motives; so it's really at the next remove, you see. Take for example the Oedipus complex, which we think is very fundamental and possibly even inborn—we don't know exactly about that—but anyhow very fundamental, a fundamental tendency. Well now, you look at a society, say particularly a German society where the father is very important, lays down the law, etc. Very well. You would expect to get an Oedipus complex there. However, what about other societies where that is less so? What about America, where the mother is more important than the father, where the "Mom" is really *the person?* Or what about still more matrilineal societies where the woman ranks very highly indeed? What about native societies where the father doesn't live with the mother and only visits her occasionally, where she lives with her brother and the boy is brought up by this brother, his uncle. What about them?

Well now, you are going to call that a cultural, environmental influence. All right, you can, but that causes naturally a shift in the form taken by your biological reactions; it's like a pressure. In the case of that last society, for instance, the boy will react to his uncle with jealousy, rivalry, opposition, hatred, and love as well, as he normally would toward the father. And his real father, who only comes in occasionally, plays with him and is his comrade in games and fun but has no authority over him, will correspond with our uncles or grandparents who spoil the child. In other words, it causes that shift. It doesn't alter the biological pattern; it only alters the form it takes.

Dr. Evans: To refer to the biological pattern in Dr. Freud's concept of libido in which he seems to talk about a broad, psychic sexual energy, there is a question as to how we should interpret the term "sex" here. Are we talking about *narrow* sexuality, or is this broad sexual drive he is talking about merely the total involvement of all biological drives? In other words, are those individuals who have suggested that he tried to explain everything in terms of repressed sexuality unfair to Freud?

Dr. Jones: Trying to explain everything in terms of repressed sexuality? I think that's going very wildly astray, don't you? He thought that the libidinal drives were a part of the biological inheritance of man, just as other instincts are, like curiosity or perhaps aggression, etc.; and he found by experience that this often enters into conflict with other aspects of the personality, which we know quite well is true and gets people into trouble in consequence. But I don't quite see—it would be ridiculous to say that some people explained everything in terms of sex, because if it were as simple as that, what would happen to his whole theory of conflict? There are two sides.

Dr. Evans: Would this be a fair statement of the situation? With his patients in the repressed culture of Vienna, Dr. Freud very often saw conflicts centered around sexuality. Therefore, in these particular patients he saw sexual conflicts as fundamental to their neuroses, which could account, at least in part, for the great emphasis on sexuality as a causative factor to be seen in his reporting. He might actually have been willing to see other underlying causes if they had been visible.

Dr. Jones: Yes, I think he would have been willing to see anything that was there.

Dr. Evans: This, of course, has been one of the bases for much criticism of Dr. Freud.

Dr. Jones: Yes, you would expect that, because by his theory there is a great deal of repression of sexuality; and naturally, if you point that out, you are bound to run into the repression, aren't you? This would illustrate what we call resistance, or opposition, or criticism, or anything you like.

Dr. Evans: To go further, Freud's interesting paper on psychopathology in everyday life revealed how Dr. Freud rather ingeniously and brilliantly could analyze any number of specific situations in just day-to-day living, seeing into the operation of the unconscious. Would Freud have said that everything we do is determined in this way? Can we ever relax and assume that some things are done merely by accident, or do we have to assume . . .

Dr. Jones: What do you mean "by accident"? If something falls from the ceiling on your foot, it would be an accident.

Dr. Evans: Would Dr. Freud have said that things which would appear to have been accidental really were not? Does one assume that there is always some unconscious involvement?

Dr. Jones: It is quite simple. Freud says all our spontaneous activity is motivated, broadly speaking. That's what you mean; none of it is accidental. No, it would be very unscientific to think it could be.

Dr. Evans: Moving along to quite a different area, Dr. Jones, one of the problems that interests us a great deal today in the United States is the one of man's overconformity. We are asking ourselves such questions as: Are we losing individual identity? Is the individual more or less becoming, as one American writer has said, "other-directed?" Are we worried so much about what the other person thinks that we don't develop truly individual personalities?

This has been commented on rather extensively by Otto Rank and Erich Fromm, who have tried to suggest that maybe the real fulfillment of man is the development of a sort of creative spirit; otherwise, we become so enmeshed in cultural social pressures that we are somewhat like machines functioning in culture, thus not true individuals. Do you feel that this view of perhaps a large segment of men in Western society is an accurate one? Is man becoming . . .

Dr. Jones: Well, I don't know what he is "becoming," but it seems to me that the state of affairs you point to is universal and eternal; that is to say, there always must have been conflict between the individual's desire to act freely without taking into regard anybody else, and the necessity he recognizes to take other people into consideration. Obviously a community would be impossible if everybody did exactly whatever he liked.

Dr. Evans: We need some order, of course, some organization.

Dr. Jones: Yes, and that is how civilization clearly evolves. I take it there has always been that conflict between the two sides. Sir Herbert Spencer was a man who wrote a great deal about that, the individual versus the State, etc. And Professor Fluegel, a follower of Spencer, wrote some very interesting essays on the same thing. Also, Freud's work essentially points to that state of conflict between the two. His book on group psychology points that out, to mention one example (7).

Then you say, "Is man becoming more conforming?" No, I should think less, because originally he must have been very conforming, if we go back to primeval man. Think now about when man first used tools, say stone tools. He struck one against the other and made it flake so that the thing would be sharp on one side, and then he used it. It took him nearly half a million years before he thought of grinding the part to make it sharp. Now, my suspicion is that a good many people tried grinding as a sharpening technique during that half a million years, and were killed for not conforming to the older pattern. So it took thousands and thousands of years before ultimately a society became so free that the members were allowed to file a bit of stone. Well now, I think we are getting freer and freer in that way. We are certainly allowed to do many things that we couldn't in the middle ages, for instance, say 120 years ago.

Of course, the extent to which free development of individuality can take place must vary in different cultures and in different periods, and that raises the very interesting problem as to why. Look at the complaint in the United States in the present, that they are going through a bad patch; that is to say, people are not allowed to develop freely. That may be true as far as I know, but the other side has its problems too.

It is generally thought that in France there is more individual development and less conforming; they don't even pay their taxes very often there. They can't get a stable government. Everyone wants to act on their own. That has its advantages, no doubt, in that it allows freer development of the individual, but it leads to practical troubles from a social point of view.

In America, I don't really know. I suppose in the small town places, places like Sinclair Lewis describes in *Main Street* and *Babbitt*, there must be a good deal of conforming. I should think the obvious factor in determining on which side the accent is placed, say in the French way of life versus the American, is probably a matter of social penalty. Now, if a man in France doesn't conform, does anything very awful happen to him? Not really. However, if a man doesn't conform in America, a lot of very awful things do happen to him. He loses his job and is not allowed to get another; or he is thrown out of the university. A whole lot of things can happen to him, and that increases the necessity to conform.

Dr. Evans: In a sense, then, you feel that immediate social pressures are forcing the individual to conform, but in the long-range, historical perspective, man is actually becoming freer and freer, more of an individual. These particular pressures to which man is subject are only momentarily relevant.

Dr. Jones: Yes, and so all over Europe in the same way. I suppose the freest place was Russia in Czarist times, provided you didn't talk about politics. You could have ideas or behavior in any direction you liked, sexually or otherwise. There was a great deal of freedom, much more so than any other country in Europe, provided you left politics out of it and didn't want to remove the

Czar. Now that is all changed. In another hundred years, however, we'll round-about again. In other words, there are constant shifts, about every fifty years or so in different countries.

Dr. Evans: Would you say that the process of undergoing psychoanalysis in a very broad sense bears on this? In other words, would you say that an individual who has sort of lost his identity by over-conforming and being too afraid of social pressures, who is disturbed and unhappy, through analysis might come to realize individual trends in himself more and perhaps become a more productive, creative individual?

Dr. Jones: Bound to. That's the aim of analysis, isn't it? The aim of analysis is to make the person more himself; that is to say, to make him the whole of "himself," not only the visible part, but the repressed part, the hidden part, the part in conflict. They should all come into play and be under a unified control so that he would be a bigger, fuller, more complete personality.

Dr. Evans: Doesn't this unified control of which you speak necessarily imply control which is social in origin?

Dr. Jones: No. I'm talking about his own conscience, and his own conscience is a thing that develops only partly from social sources, social control, etc. As you know, he begins very much earlier in life, and his conscience goes back at least to the first year of life. You can trace the beginning of it.

Dr. Evans: The first impact of the small family structure on the neophyte.

Dr. Jones: Yes, and possibly even inborn tendencies.

Dr. Evans: What exactly is the nature of these inborn tendencies bearing on social morality to which Freud referred as the "Super-ego"? Are we to believe that man is already born with built-in prohibitions on his social existence?

Dr. Jones: It is hard to prove or demonstrate things of that sort. I should think myself it is very likely, because I don't think that all of the super-ego comes from the outside pressure. I think some comes from inside. The child is born with much wilder impulses than we have when we are grown up. He not only has to learn to control them and guide them in certain directions for social reasons, but also for personal reasons, because some of them are very harmful to himself, very destructive to himself, or destructive to somebody he loves. In other words, there are dangers coming from within as well as from without; so there is a necessity to control or repress, or to do something about those internal dangers. It seems very likely to me that that control is inborn, for biological reasons of survival.

Dr. Evans: Now in terms of a climate of conformity as opposed to a climate of greater freedom, would you comment upon what effect these different climates might have upon productivity, creativity, and perhaps even genius among a given people? Would people like Beethoven, for instance, have emerged in a climate of conformity? Is it possible that a Van Gogh could have been produced in a climate of conformity? Or even a Freud?

Dr. Jones: Freud was certainly brought up in a climate of conformity, wasn't he?

Dr. Evans: So what are the ingredients that allow an individual who is brought up in a very conforming climate to show amazingly unique individuality in creative efforts? This is the sort of thing that gets into the whole problem of what actually are the ingredients of genius.

Dr. Jones: We would very much like to know that. There are two sides to that. You do see creative work being produced in apparently unfavorable circumstances, in what you call a "conformist environment," and the thing thrusts through, willy-nilly. Right!

However, you also see on the other hand that it becomes more frequent in certain periods. Take the Renaissance period of Italy when you had great painters and artists, sculptors and architects right and left all over the place simply flourishing. One thinks that the climate of opinion then must have been favorable to that creativity, much more so than in many other times. At the present the time is favorable, no doubt, to scientific inventions and discoveries.

Dr. Evans: So even individual, creative genius must

come forth in a social structure conducive to its emergence. For example, in the case of Dr. Freud, the period was one in which there was favorable reaction to work in neurology, the research of Breuer, and the work of some French psychiatrists. Would you agree in the case of Freud that he produced in a period, characterized by a scientific setting that lent itself readily to such creative expression?

Dr. Jones: No, I don't think so in that case at all. I think it was one of those rare cases where you wouldn't expect anything. There was nothing in Vienna to favor that in the very least, you see. There was that one little episode ten years before when Freud became acquainted with Herr Breuer and his work, but I think Freud had mostly forgotten about it and had not made much of it. Later on it was picked up and woven into the work he was doing.

Dr. Evans: So he didn't continually seem to feel the impact of Breuer at all . . .

Dr. Jones: None, not at all. He learned about the Breuer case in 1882, but Freud was a neurologist way up to the nineties before he even started the psychological side. No, I should think that Vienna was a non-favorable, very unfavorable environment, very much a conformist environment.

Dr. Evans: So in a sense then, you're suggesting that the generalization that a great genius can't emerge from a conformist environment is an extreme over-simplification, that we just can't speak meaningfully in these terms.

Dr. Jones: Well, yes. I suppose it's a relative matter. You can put it in terms of pressure. If the move toward creative genius is strong enough, it will burst through in conformity; and if the conformity is not very strong, such as in Italy during the Renaissance, it gets through more easily. It is merely a relative matter.

Dr. Evans: In this general area, we have read with great interest your analyses of literary figures such as Hamlet in Shakespeare. There has been a very interesting tendency in literary circles to apply psychoanalytic theory to an understanding or evaluation of great literature.

Does it follow that the young writer should study psychoanalytic theory? Would this be of help to him?
Should the critic become thoroughly acquainted with
these ideas also?

Dr. Jones: I think there is a sharp distinction between
the writer and the critic. I would say "no" for one and
"yes" for the other. I think the writer would be harmed
if he tried to benefit by psychoanalytic knowledge, because he would be harmed if he tried to benefit by any
knowledge from outside himself and how he personally
feels about things, say political knowledge or what
not; it would take away from his own spontaneous impulses. The more spontaneous the writer, the greater the
writer. The creation must come from within. If he
started merely copying, looking up things in a textbook
and saying, "Now that's the proper thing to say," he
would not really be bringing out anything that's worthwhile. I'm quite definite about that. On the other hand,
when it comes to the critic, this internal aspect of the
problem is not really important.

Dr. Evans: With respect to the use of psychoanalytic
theory and understanding, you have commented that
with the author it may actually be a stifling thing. It
may not allow him to free his individuality adequately.
On the other hand, you suggested that with a critic this
may be a different matter.

Dr. Jones: Quite different. But let me be quite clear
in what I mean about the writer before we discuss the
critic. I didn't mean to say that being analyzed would
be harmful to the writer, but rather that reading about
it would be harmful. I meant that if a writer should be
analyzed, he would be a freer, fuller writer; he would be
clearer and more spontaneous.

With the critic, however, it's different again, because
I think all the way around psychoanalytic knowledge can
be helpful to the critic. The critic's job is to assess both
the aesthetic side of the work that he is reviewing or
criticizing, and also the intellectual content. The aesthetic evaluation depends, of course, upon the critic's
sensibility, which implies the need for freedom of his feelings; and where the intellectual analysis of the content is

concerned, I think a knowledge of psychoanalysis is very helpful, enabling the person to more accurately estimate how consistent the production is. Now take the case of "Hamlet"; that was a play that was relevant on many different levels. It probably had a current political reference, perhaps forgotten now. There were all sorts of social allusions at that time, peculiar to the specific period of the play, which people then could understand; there were particular jokes maybe, different layers, until you got deeper and deeper, and the whole thing became unified. Now if any production is a really great work of art, it is consistent all the way through; and when I say consistent, I mean it's true all the way through. That, I think, a critic ought to be able to evaluate.

Dr. Evans: A certain intrinsic unity in the over-all analysis.

Dr. Jones: Yes.

Dr. Evans: This has become rather a "favorite pastime" of some, to look at characters in literature in this manner. Of course, I think your contribution more or less became a pioneer focus for this type of thinking.

Dr. Jones: Yes. However, they can also go wrong when they merely translate. They translate into this complex or that complex, and I don't think that gets you very far. Anybody can do that.

Dr. Evans: It is too superficial.

Dr. Jones: When you simply learn, you have gained merely superficial knowledge. I think that is a very different thing from understanding the dynamics.

Dr. Evans: Dr. Jones, a very interesting question, one brought to mind by your biography of Dr. Freud, concerns the impact of a genius's own personal life on what he produces. For example, there has been much research in recent years in which there has been some attempt to study the basic personality of individuals in the hope that what leads them into various professions or into various productive efforts can be ascertained. In fact, Freud himself with his analysis of DaVinci suggests that we can in a very deterministic type of analysis understand how an individual may produce, the basic foundation upon which production rests. Now in the case of Freud's own personal life, in what way do you feel his life may have influenced the direction of his psychoanalytic theories and the formulations therein?

Dr. Jones: Well, there again we've got to distinguish. I think the main direction in which he was influenced was from the point of view of interest; certain things led him to take an interest in this, that, and the other. That's one thing. Now another consideration inherent in your question concerns the actual formulation of his various scientific theories. And then there is also a third thing; that is, to what extent his personal penchant, his own general outlook on life, served as an influence on him. Those are three quite different things. Which shall we take first now?

I should think that there must be ultimately some form of curiosity, surely. Why curiosity should take that particular direction would depend probably on more delicate infantile influences than are easy to put your finger on now. But as regards any personal influences acting on his theories, I am really not aware of that. I should say that his theories were objective and originated as a result of his experience. He came across certain facts, and he tried to group them as every scientist does; he tried to provide a unifying hypothesis for them. Of course, it is obvious that his personal experiences must have influenced him a great deal in his general outlook on life. For instance, he was an atheist. That must have been due to something in his early life. He was never brought up with a strong religious influence, so it may have been easy for him to do without it. What other things can we say?

Dr. Evans: Well, for example, let us take the fact that his father was so much older than his mother. Do you think it possible that this age differential might be discernible in some of his formulations?

Dr. Jones: I think that made it harder for him to recognize the Oedipus situation. He was very fond of his father, and they got along very well, being of similar types of mind. His father was a free-thinking, humorous, witty, liberal-minded type of man, just like Freud. Freud had an extraordinary sense of humor, and was very fond of jokes, etc. Most of this, he got from his father. Thus, to discover that there was within him a secret hatred of his father must have been very difficult.

Dr. Evans: Some writers have said that one reason Dr. Freud was able to probe so deeply into human personality and see the worst in man is that underneath he really had a deep hatred of man.

Dr. Jones: One can form an estimate and say, "Well, I think man's a pretty poor creature; he's got this, that, and the other defect about him," and so to speak, make an intellectual judgment. That's a different thing than an emotional attitude from which might stem such statements as, "I hate all men," or "I love all men." One thinks that both of these extremes are abnormal. A man who says, "I hate every man," or a man who says, "I love every man," must have something wrong with him in either case. In other words, there is nothing objective about this kind of an emotional evaluation, and I don't think that Freud was that lacking in objectivity.

He had the same unwillingness to see some of the things he was uncovering through his work—recognition of infantile sexuality, Oedipus complexes, etc.—as anybody else. In fact, he may have been even more unwilling to see these things than many, because he was a very, shall I say, respectable person, very chaste and puritanical by nature at that time in his life. No doubt, his ideas got freer later as he found out more about human nature.

About loving, however, there was something special where Freud was concerned, though I don't think it influenced his theories much. I think he tended to like people he met, and tended to expect and hope for more than he got; he was inclined to think that each new fellow he met was a fine fellow, wonderful in all respects. Then, of course, when his expectations weren't met, he would be disappointed and drop the fellow, and he would feel badly about it.

Dr. Evans: In short, a sort of disillusionment.

Dr. Jones: Yes, disillusionment. He rather prepared for disillusionment. Of course, his relationship with Jung is an obvious example. He thought very highly of Jung, thought the world of him, and then he was disillusioned.

He went flat. That was a peculiarity of Freud, but I don't think that it influenced his actual work or theories at all.

Dr. Evans: Do you feel that he was able to more or less separate in actuality the personal from what he produced?

Dr. Jones: Yes, very much.

Dr. Evans: I know that in some of his later work he became, in the opinion of some, more speculative than scientific with his discussions of such things as religion and war. Do you think that Freud's work could be better understood if we could separate this type of speculation from his more fundamental observations?

Dr. Jones: Yes, very definitely.

Dr. Evans: When can we say that Freud's work became more a reflection of personal ideology, as opposed to an earlier time when it can be described as more scientific and objective?

Dr. Jones: I think that there is a very sharp point at which we can make this distinction, the year after the end of the First War, the year 1919, when he was writing the book, *Beyond the Pleasure Principle* (8). In this book he was getting into philosophy over his conception of the death instinct. You see, the death instinct was supposed to be not only a human thing, but a concept that applied to all living matter. There was an inherent tendency toward self-destruction, not only in all animals, but in vegetables as well. Now one has to say that that is not a biological conception, and one also has to say, strictly speaking, that it is not a scientific one. It's an idea like any other philosophical idea. I think that period in Freud's career marks the beginning of the ideological tone to which you referred. You can trace several things after that probably, but they are always all mixed up, aren't they? I mean, he was a rationalist, which means he tried to take an objective stand in viewing this, that, and the other, rather than depending on intuition or emotion. So with respect to his books on group psychology, even those which fell in that period, I think you've got to take into account the rational aspect, which is really the scientific part, as well as his personal outlook. It's not all personal.

Dr. Evans: In some of his later works on mental telepathy, clairvoyance, and so on, could their contents be classified under the realm of his genuinely empirical research?

Dr. Jones: No, not a bit. That's purely personal. I mean, he considered, or it was his opinion, that there was sufficient evidence to hold such and such a belief. Very well. Whether or not one considers the evidence sufficient in a given case to draw conclusions cannot, in the final analysis, be entirely objective. You nearly always are influenced for or against by some prejudice or emotional element stemming from your background. In Freud's case, there was a tendency to believe, and also a tendency to doubt. It is very interesting that in his different statements one could see certain alternations. There was both a sort of credulous attitude and a skeptical attitude. Undoubtedly, he had both.

Dr. Evans: Referring again to the influence of one's personal philosophy or ideology on one's creativity, we, of course, are aware that there was considerable anti-Semitism in the area in which Freud lived; and following from that, there are many people who tend to associate sexual theories with Judaism, and so on.

Dr. Jones: Like Hitler? I believe *he* did.

Dr. Evans: Was Freud aware of anti-Semitism in so deep a sense that it troubled him?

Dr. Jones: Yes, I should say probably yes. (I *should* say no.) He encountered it in pretty strong form at different times. He wasn't given a title at the University for years and years and years; he was turned down every time.

In some of the earlier experiences of his life which I know about, I know that he was set upon in fun. And yes, I think he was a sensitive man, a very sensitive man, one that probably thought a lot and asked, "Why is all this?" I'm sure he wondered, "What is there that is so peculiar about us? People don't sit on other people like that." These feelings, of course, are what led him to write his last book, *Moses and Monotheism* (9). It's all about the nature of Judaism. I expect you are right; he had been aware of anti-Semitism all his life.

Dr. Evans: To go a little further into this general problem, you touched upon a point which I think is very interesting. You appeared to suggest that Freud came from a fairly puritanical type of background, and that he himself was probably, in a moral sense, rather puritanical. Would this be correct?

Dr. Jones: No. I shouldn't have said his background. What I should have said is that he was more moral and puritanical than his background. His mother was very easygoing, free and easy. No doubt she was moral in her behavior, as far as I know certainly, but I wouldn't have called her a puritanical person.

Dr. Evans: It's rather strange, the distortion of a man's point of view and of his theories which occurs when they are subjected to various interpretations. You encounter it so often. For example, there were many people who became horrified over Freud's theories, because they believed that his theories more or less preached free love, and that monogamy was inconsistent with psychoanalytic doctrine, that we shouldn't repress sexual drives lest we become neurotic, and so on. I wonder if Freud was aware of these misconceptions?

Dr. Jones: Of course he was. Also, he was aware of how much of the content of his work was being ascribed to the local atmosphere in Vienna, which he thought was peculiarly silly. You see, if it was actually true, and this I don't know, that the Viennese mode of life was freer than at other places such as Berlin or London, then it would be the last place where you would discover repression. Freud said to me once, "I always thought that that particular accusation must cover another one; it's the Jewish environment that they really mean."

Dr. Evans: To leave this general problem of one's personal philosophy upon his work, a question that is very much the center of controversy, particularly in the United States and to some extent in England, is one of the amount of freedom our children should be allowed as they grow up. We have some extremes on this issue.

We have one extreme which follows the disciplinarian approach that historically has been part of most of our cultures. Utilizing this approach, we control the child almost completely and give him very little freedom.

Then, of course, the other extreme has been a very permissive approach where we allow the child to develop his individuality, attempting to force upon him absolutely no restrictions or frustrating demands whatsoever. As a result of this approach, we have seen in many of our households children behaving in a destructive and anti-social manner with parents who tolerate this poor behavior because they fear they may frustrate their children. Unfortunately, particularly in the United States, many individuals have blamed psychoanalysis—

Dr. Jones: For both of them?

Dr. Evans: For suggesting the unrestrained view. In fact, many laymen have referred to the "psychological approach" as a product of Freud's work. I wonder if you might comment upon how Freud actually viewed this problem?

Dr. Jones: He would recognize that frustrations are an inevitable part of living in a community. There must be frustrations. Nobody can do absolutely everything he likes. He can't go and defecate in the street, and limitations such as that begin as early in life as infancy. The infant has external frustrations, such as only being allowed his mother's breast on certain occasions. Frustrations like these are inevitable. The mother isn't always in the same room; sometimes when the child cries for her, she is in another room, another inevitable frustration.

Also, there are inevitable frustrations in social life, which an individual must encounter. Now, the extent to which he experiences difficulty with these social frustrations we think depends upon the varying ease or difficulty he has in tolerating them. The point is that abolishing frustrations isn't the answer; you must learn to tolerate them.

Dr. Evans: So it was Freud's psychoanalytic view, and certainly it is your view, that in order to develop frustration tolerance, the developing child must be exposed to some frustrations.

Dr. Jones: Well, you are exposed to them anyway, and you are overlooking that when you talk about freedom.

Dr. Evans: Along the same line, a very interesting writer in the United States, Dr. David Levy, has postulated that there is an unfortunate tendency for an increasing number of mothers to over-protect their children. This over-protection which takes many forms essentially prolongs the infantilism of the child. Looking at this matter, would you say that it is primarily a cultural pattern, one that might have emerged, for instance, from American culture, not necessarily indicating any innate tendency in the mother? Or would you say that there is an innate tendency to over-protect in all mothers in all cultures?

Dr. Jones: I should say that there is a tendency for all mothers to over-protect. She, in fact, gets into a certain amount of conflict over this tendency, because as the child emerges into adult life, he doesn't need that kind of protection, forcing her to give up some of the manifestations of this tendency. It is not always easy for her.

Dr. Evans: So this is something that possibly would not be typical to any particular culture?

Dr. Jones: Surely it is not peculiar to any culture, but it probably does vary in strengths in different cultures. It can, of course, be furthered by certain social attitudes. I think there has been more of this tendency in America, for example, than in Germany; but again, the thing on which it is based is biological. It is there; it can be furthered or checked, but it can't be created by any cultural thing.

Dr. Evans: Now, let us address ourselves to the problem of the treatment of mental disorders. In addition to the pioneer technique of psychoanalysis, various other types of techniques for treatment of these disorders have been developed. Among these are shock therapy, psychosurgery, variations of the original psychoanalytic approach, and so on.

One of the most recent developments has been the

use of tranquilizing drugs. In fact, the first one, chlor-promazine, was first used here in France. Since then, many milder tranquilizers have been developed which are being dispensed by physicians on quite a large scale. How do you view this practice?

Dr. Jones: It's like sitting on a steam safety valve. Of course you can dampen it down. If you want to, you can give a drug that will make a person unconscious; give enough opium and you can dampen anything down. The same principle is involved in lowering the degree of tension with barbituates, or what not. You can lower the degree of tension in the individual, but you aren't changing anything. Whatever caused the tension is still there. If you take away the drug, it comes back again. I don't think there is any evidence to show that any drug can change either the personality or the content of particular conflicts or ideas which may be disturbing the individual.

Dr. Evans: One view has been that certain types of seriously ill psychotic patients such as the schizophrenic with whom the psychotherapist is simply unable to communicate become more amenable to therapy through use of drugs. Under these conditions do you think the use of drugs is in order?

Dr. Jones: No, I don't think it is very helpful. Is there value in the patient becoming more amenable, let us say, to psychoanalytic therapy? No, I don't think so, because when you dampen the emotions in that way, you're making them less accessible to change; and, of course, changing them is your aim. You have to get hold of a thing before you can handle it, before you can change it. By temporarily abolishing it, you are no further along.

Dr. Evans: In other words, although it may appear to be a way of making the patient more accessible, it really is making him less so?

Dr. Jones: That's correct; it makes him less accessible.

Dr. Evans: Now, of course, all of this reflects new developments in treating much more seriously disturbed patients, such as the psychotic.

Dr. Jones: It then becomes a practical matter, just like

strait jackets in the old days—a practical matter; tie them up.

Dr. Evans: Now another important problem, articulated not so long ago by Julian Huxley, deals with the conflict between the extreme advances in man's technological development and his very limited socio-psychological development. For example, means have been created technologically that could destroy all mankind, while our socio-psychological development, our ability in human relations, has not come far enough to insure us against such an event.

Dr. Jones: Yes, I've written something on that very matter. As a matter of fact, the third volume of my Freud biography finishes on that note, so please allow me to read the final paragraphs. They deal with those two fundamental instincts that Freud worked on so much— the sexual and the aggressive:

"When we consider the breath-taking achievements of man in art and in science, we must judge there are no limits foreseeable to his power to attain happiness and security. But this vision is offset by one as somber as that is glowing. In it are three main strands. The advances in medical science, which are now bound to continue rapidly, combined with the increase in general prosperity, have diminished the natural selection of quality. They have also brought about such an enormous increase in quantity of population that the time cannot be far distant when the resources of the earth to sustain it will be seriously strained. Moreover, greed and lack of foresight have not only failed to nourish those resources, ultimately the soil and the minerals of the earth's crust, but are ruining them at a truly alarming pace. Still graver is the consideration that man's destructive powers have been so fortified by the recently acquired knowledge of new weapons that it is now within his reach to achieve devastation beside which the efforts of an Attila, a Timurlane or a Genghis Khan are but the puny gestures of an infant. It is now no longer massacre that is threatened, but the possible extinction of all life on this planet. There needs only a madman in the seat of authority of the kind we have just witnessed to set this holocaust ablaze, nor can we be sure that someone less mad may not bring it about.

"Amid the turmoil of conflicting ideas in which we live, in the spheres of art, of science, and above all of politics where statesmen of towering importance can display in their savagery, fear and unreasonableness, all the worst features of an undisciplined nursery, there seems to be one proposition commanding nearly universal assent. The control man has secured over nature has far outrun his control over himself. Man's unhappiness and the threats of doom overhanging him proceed from this unassailable truth. Man's chief enemy and danger is his own unruly nature and the dark forces pent up within him.

"If our race is lucky enough to survive for another thousand years, the name of Sigmund Freud will be remembered as that of the man who first ascertained the origin and nature of those forces, and pointed the way to achieving some measure of control over them (15)."

References

1. Allport, G. W. *Becoming: Basic Considerations for a Psychology of Personality.* New Haven: Yale University Press, 1954.
2. ———. *Pattern and Growth in Personality.* New York: Holt, Rinehart & Winston, 1961.
3. Arendt, H. *Eichmann in Jerusalem.* New York: Viking Press, 1963.
4. Bandura, A., and Walters, R. H. *Social Learning and Personality Development.* New York: Holt, Rinehart & Winston, 1963.
5. Bernfeld, S., and Feitelberg, S. "Bericht über einige psychophysiologische Arbeiten," *Imago,* XX (1934), 224.
6. Camus, A. *The Stranger.* Translated by Stuart Gilbert. New York: Alfred A. Knopf, 1946.

7. Carson, R. L. *Silent Spring.* Boston: Houghton Mifflin, 1962.

8. Erikson, E. H. *Young Man Luther: A Study in Psychoanalysis and History.* New York: W. W. Norton, 1958.

9. ———. "The Roots of Virtue," in *The Humanist Frame.* J. Huxley (ed.). New York: Harper & Row, 1961. Pp. 145–66.

10. ———. *Childhood and Society.* New York: W. W. Norton, 1950. Second enlarged edition, 1963.

11. ———. "The Golden Rule and the Cycle of Life," in *The Study of Lives.* R. W. White (ed.). New York: Appleton-Century-Crofts, 1963.

12. ———. *Insight and Responsibility.* New York: W. W. Norton, 1964.

13. ———. "Gandhi's Autobiography: The Leader as a Child," *The American Scholar,* Autumn, 1966.

14. ———. "The Ontogeny of Ritualization in Man," *Proceedings of the Royal Society.* London (in press).

15. Erikson, K. "Patient Role and Social Uncertainty," *Psychiatry,* XX (1957), 263–74.

16. Evans, R. I. *Conversations with Carl Jung and Reactions from Ernest Jones.* New York: D. Van Nostrand, 1964.

17. ———. *Dialogue with Erich Fromm.* New York: Harper & Row, 1966.

18. ———. "A New Interdisciplinary Dimension in Graduate Psychological Research Training: Dentistry," *Amer. Psychol.,* Vol. XXI, No. 2 (1966), pp. 167–72.

19. Freud, A. *The Ego and the Mechanism of Defense.* New York: International Universities Press, 1946.

20. Fromm, E. *Man for Himself.* New York: Rinehart, 1947.

21. ———. *Psychoanalysis and Religion.* New Haven, Conn.: Yale University Press, 1950.

22. ———. *The Art of Loving.* New York: Harper & Brothers, 1956.

23. Gandhi, M. K. *An Autobiography or the Story of My Experiments with Truth*. Ahmedabad, India: Navjivan Publishing House, 1945.

24. Hartmann, H. *Psychoanalysis and Moral Values*. New York: International Universities Press, 1960.

25. Heidegger, M. *An Introduction to Metaphysics*. Translated by Ralph Manheim. New Haven, Conn.: Yale University Press, 1959.

26. Horney, K. *The Neurotic Personality of Our Time*. New York: W. W. Norton, 1937.

27. Husserl, E. *Ideas: General Introduction to Pure Phenomenology*. Translated by W. R. Boyce Gibson. New York: Macmillan, 1952.

28. Huxley, J. (ed.). *The Humanist Frame*. New York: Harper & Row, 1961.

29. Kardiner, A. *The Individual and his Society*. New York: Columbia University Press, 1939.

30. Malinowski, B. *Sex and Repression in Savage Society*. New York: Harcourt, Brace, 1927.

31. Maslow, A. H. *Motivation and Personality*. New York: Harper & Brothers, 1954.

32. May, Rollo. "Existential Bases of Psychotherapy," in *Existential Psychology*. Rollo May (ed.). New York: Random House, 1961.

33. McClelland, D. C. *Personality*. New York: William Sloan Associates, 1951.

34. McCurdy, H. G. *The Personal World: An Introduction to the Study of Personality*. New York: Harcourt, Brace & World, Inc., 1961.

35. Piaget, J. *The Psychology of Intelligence*. Translated by M. Piercy and D. E. Berlyne. London: Routledge and Kegan Paul, 1950.

36. Rank, O. *Will Therapy and Truth and Reality*. Translated by Jessie Taft. New York: Alfred A. Knopf, 1945.

37. Rogers, C. R. *Casebook of Non-Directive Counseling.* Boston: Houghton Mifflin, 1947.
38. Rokeach, M. *The Three Christs of Ypsilanti.* New York: Alfred A. Knopf, 1964.
39. Sanford, N. "Will Psychologists Study Human Problems?", *Amer. Psychol.,* Vol. XX, No. 3 (1965), pp. 192–202.
40. Skinner, B. F., Solomon, H. C., and Lindsley O. R. "A New Method for the Experimental Analysis of the Behavior of Psychotic Patients," *J. Nervous Mental Diseases,* CXX (1954), 403–6.
41. Sullivan, H. S. *The Interpersonal Theory of Psychiatry.* New York: W. W. Norton, 1953.
42. Tillich, P. *The Courage to Be.* New Haven, Conn.: Yale University Press, 1952.
43. White, R. W. *Lives in Progress.* New York: Dryden Press, 1952.
44. ———. "Motivation Reconsidered: The Concept of Competence," *Psych. Rev.,* LXVI (1959), 297–333.
45. Wolpe, J. *Psychotherapy by Reciprocal Inhibition.* Stanford, Calif.: Stanford University Press, 1958.

Bibliography*

ERIK H. ERIKSON

Original Writings

1930. "Die Zukunft der Aufklärung und die Psychoanalyse,"
Zeitschrift der Psychoanalytik Paedagogie, IV (1930),
201–16.

1931a. "Psychoanalysis and the Future of Education," *Psychoanal. Quart.*, IV (1935), 50–68.

1931b. "Bilderbücher," *Zeitschrift der Psychoanalytik Paedagogie*, V (1931), 13–19.

1937a. "Configurations in Play: Clinical Notes," *Psychoanal.
Quart.*, VI (1937), 139–214.

1937b. "Traumatische Konfigurationen im Spiel," *Imago*,
XXIII (1937), 447–516.

* Listings are arranged by year of original publication.

Bibliography

1939. "Observations on Sioux Education," *J. Psychol.*, VII (1939), 101–56.

1940a. "Problems of Infancy and Early Childhood," in P. G. Davis (ed.), *The Cyclopedia of Medicine*, XII: *Surgery and Specialties*, pp. 714–30. Philadelphia: F. A. Davis, 1940.

1940b. "Studies in the Interpretation of Play: 1–Clinical Observation of Play Disruption in Young Children, *Genet. Psychol. Monogr.*, XXII (1940), 557–671.

1941. "Further Explorations in Play Construction," *Psychol. Bull.*, XXXVIII (1941), 748.

1942. "Hitler's Imagery and German Youth," *Psychiat.*, V (1942), 475–93.

1943a. "Observations on the Yurok: Childhood and World Image," *Amer. Archaeol. Ethnol.*, Vol. XXXV, No. 10 (1943), pp. 257–301.

1943b. "Clinical Studies in Childhood Play," in R. C. Barker, *et al.*, *Child Behavior and Development*. New York: McGraw-Hill, 1943, pp. 411–28.

1945a. "Childhood and Tradition in Two American Indian Tribes," in O. Fenichel, *et al.* (eds.), *The Psychoanalytic Study of the Child*, I, 319–50. New York: International Universities Press, 1945.

1945b. "Plans for the Veteran with Symptoms of Instability," in Louise Wirth, *Community Planning for Peacetime Living*. Palo Alto, Calif.: Stanford University Press, 1945.

1946. "Ego Development and Historical Change," in Phillis Greenacre, *et al.* (eds.), *The Psychoanalytic Study of the Child*, II, 359–96. New York: International Universities Press, 1946.

1949. "Ruth Benedict," A. L. Kroeber (ed.), *Ruth Fulton Benedict: A Memorial*. New York: Viking Fund, 1949.

152 /

1950a. *Childhood and Society.* New York: W. W. Norton, 1950.

1950b. In M. J. E. Senn (ed.), "Growth and Crises of the Healthy Personality," *Symposium on the Healthy Personality,* pp. 91–146. New York: Josiah Macy, Jr. Foundation, 1950.

1951a. "Sex Differences in the Play Configuration of Pre-Adolescents," *Amer. J. Orthopsychiat.,* Vol. XXI, No. 4 (1951), pp. 667–92.

1951b. "Statement to the Committee on Privilege and Tenure of the University of California on the California Loyalty Oath: An Editorial," *Psychiat.,* Vol. XIV, No. 3 (1951), pp. 244–5.

1952. Remarks, in *Healthy Personality Development in Children as Related to Programs of the Federal Government,* pp. 80–95. New York: Josiah Macy, Jr. Foundation, 1952.

1953. "On the Sense of Inner Identity," in *Conference on Health and Human Relations,* pp. 124–46. New York: McGraw-Hill, 1953.

1954a. *Juvenile Delinquency.* Paper read at a teaching seminar, Pittsburgh, Department of Child Psychiatry and Child Development, University of Pittsburgh, 1954.

1954b. "Wholeness and Totality: A Psychiatric Contribution," in C. J. Friedrich (ed.), *Totalitarianism,* pp. 156–71. Cambridge, Mass.: Harvard University Press, 1954.

1954c. "The Dream Specimen of Psychoanalysis," *J. Amer. Psychoanal. Assn.,* Vol. II, No. 1 (1954), pp. 5–56.

1954d. "Identity and Totality: Psychoanalytic Observations on the Problems of Youth," *Human Developm. Bull.,* pp. 50–82. Chicago: The Human Development Student Organization, 1954.

1954e. "On the Sense of Inner Identity," in R. P. Knight and C. R. Friedman (eds.), *Psychoanalytic Psychiatry and Psychology, Clinical and Theoretical Papers, Austen Riggs Center,* 131–70. New York, International Universities Press, 1954.

1954f. "Problems of Infancy and Early Childhood," in G. Murphy and A. J. Bachrach, *Outline of Abnormal Psychology,* pp. 3–36. New York: Random House, 1954.

1954g. In B. Schaffner (ed.), *Group Processes* (Transactions of the First Conference, 1954). New York: Josiah Macy, Jr., Foundation, 1956.

1955a. In B. Schaffner (ed.), *Group Processes* (Transactions of the Second Conference, 1955). New York: Josiah Macy Jr., Foundation, 1956.

1955b. "Toys and Reasons," in Clara Thompson, *An Outline of Psychoanalysis,* pp. 227–47. New York: Random House, 1955.

1955c. "Sex Differences in the Play Configurations of American Adolescents," in Margaret Mead and Martha Wolfenstein (eds.), *Childhood in Contemporary Cultures,* pp. 324–41. Chicago: University of Chicago Press, 1955.

1955d. Freud's "The Origins of Psychoanalysis," *Int. J. Psychoanal.,* Vol. XXXVI, No. 1 (1955), pp. 1–15.

1955e. "Comments on Permissiveness." Paper read at Staff Training Institute, Department of Child Psychiatry and Child Development, University of Pittsburgh, 1955.

1956a. "Comments at a Round-Table Discussion about a Consideration of the Biological, Psychological and Cultural Approaches to the Understanding of Human Development and Behavior," in J. M. Tanner, *Discussions on*

Child Development, IV, 133–54. New York: International Universities Press, 1960.

1956b. "The Problem of Ego Identity," *J. Amer. Psychoanal. Assn.,* Vol. IV, No. 1 (1956), pp. 56–121.

1956c. "Ego Identity and the Psychosocial Moratorium," in Helen Witmer and Ruth Kotansky, *New Perspective for Research,* pp. 1–23. Washington, D.C.: U.S. Department of Health, Education, and Welfare (#356), 1956.

1956d. "The First Psychoanalyst," *Yale Review,* Autumn, 1956, pp. 40–62.

1957. "Sigmund Freud's Psychoanalytik Krise und Trieb und Umwelt in der Kindheit," in "Frankfurter Beiträge zur Sozialogie," *Freud in der Gegenwart,* pp. 10–30, 43–64. Frankfurt, Germany: Europäische Verlaganstalt, 1957.

1958a. *Young Man Luther: A Study in Psychoanalysis and History.* New York: W. W. Norton, 1958.

1958b. In J. Tanner and B. Inhelder (eds.), *Discussions on Child Development* (Comments on a Roundtable Discussion), III, 16–18, 91–215. New York: International Universities Press, 1958.

1958c. "The Nature of Clinical Evidence," *Daedalus,* Vol. XXXVII, No. 4 (1958), pp. 65–87.

1959a. "Identity and the Life Cycle: Selected Papers," *Psychol. Issues* (Monogr.), Vol. I, No. 1 (1959). New York: International Universities Press.

1959b. "Late Adolescence," in D. H. Funkenstein (ed.), *The Student and Mental Health.* New York: World Federation for Mental Health and The International Association of Universities, 1959.

1960. "Youth and the Life Cycle: An Interview," *Childr.,* Vol. VII, No. 2 (1960), pp. 43–9.

1961. "The Roots of Virtue," in J. Huxley (ed.), *The Humanist Frame*, pp. 145–66. New York: Harper & Row, 1961.

1962a. "Youth: Fidelity and Diversity," *Daedalus*, Vol. XXIX, No. 1 (1962), pp. 5–27.

1962b. "Reality and Actuality," *J. Amer. Psychoanal. Assn.*, Vol. X, No. 3 (1962), pp. 451–73.

1963a. *Youth: Change and Challenge* (ed.). New York: Basic Books, 1963.

1963b. "The Golden Rule and the Cycle of Life," in R. W. White (ed.), *The Study of Lives*, pp. 412–28. New York: Prentice-Hall, 1963.

1964a. "The Inner and the Outer Space: Reflections on Womanhood," *Daedalus*, II (1964), 582–606.

1964b. *Insight and Responsibility*. New York: W. W. Norton, 1964.

1964c. "Memorandum on Identity and Negro Youth," *J. soc. Issues*, Vol. XX, No. 4 (1964), pp. 29–42.

1965a. "Psychoanalysis and Ongoing History: Problems of Identity, Hatred and Nonviolence," *J. Amer. Psychoanal. Assn.*, CXXII (1965), 241–50.

1965b. "Concluding remarks," J. A. Mattfeld and C. G. Van Aken (eds.), *Women and the Scientific Professions*, pp. 232–45. Cambridge, Mass.: M.I.T. Press, 1965.

1966a. "The Concept of Identity in Race Relations: Notes and Queries," *Daedalus*, Vol. XCV, No. 1 (1966), pp. 145–70.

1966b. "Gandhi's Autobiography: The Leader as a Child," *The American Scholar*, Autumn, 1966.

"The Ontogeny of Ritualization in Man," *Proceedings of the Royal Society*. London (in press).

Collaborative Writings

1937. and M. Gitelson, "Play Therapy," *Amer. J. Orthopsychiat.*, Vol. VIII, No. 3 (1937), pp. 499–524.

1953. and Joan Erikson, "The Power of the Newborn," *Mademoiselle*, June, 1953, pp. 62, 100–2.

1958. and Kai T. Erikson, "The confirmation of the Delinquent," *Best Articles and Stories*, Vol. 2, No. 7 (1958), pp. 43–6.

Index

approach to, 41; "identity crisis," 6, 28, 35, 38, 41, 56; ideology as a basis for, 35; Martin Luther's problems of, 42; national, 29; "personal," 37; positive and negative elements in, 32, 35–36, 38, 40; problems of, in current era, 29; problems of, for women, 42–45, 49; psychosocial, 33, 35, 37–38; recurring problems of, in later stages, 40–41; as relatively unconscious conflict, 28; retrospective, 41; societal aspect of, 33; territoriality of, 77; versus role diffusion, 28, 30; "what works" as basis for, 33–34

"Identity and the Life Cycle: Selected Papers" (Erikson), 21n

Ideological innovators, as leaders, 69–70

Ideology, as a basis for identity, 35

Impersonality, in psychoanalysis, 104

Incorporative mode, in behavior, 14

India: and protest on salt tax, 79; psycho-historical analysis of, 64, 71–76; traditional version of life cycle in, 64

see also Gandhi, Mahatma

Individuality, 117; vs. femininity and masculinity, 46–48, 110

Industry: definition of, 28; versus inferiority, 25, 27, 28

Inferiority: as failure of attempts toward mastery, 28; feelings of, 20; versus industry, 25, 27, 28

Initiative versus guilt, 23, 24

Insight: distinction between intellectual and emotional, 90–91; in psychoanalysis, 91, 97, 100; in therapeutic relationship, 89–90

Insight and Responsibility (Erikson), 89

Instincts: biological notion of, 87; and Freudian theory, 86, 87; instinctive patterns and instinctual forces, 87; and *Trieb*, 87

Interpretation, in psychoanalysis, 31, 92, 97, 100

Intimacy: as fusing of identities, 48–49; versus isolation, 48, 50

Introspection, and psychoanalysis, 95–96, 97

Isolation, feelings of, 29, 38

Jewish psychoanalysts, 95

Johnson, Lyndon B.: as leader, 69, 70; on women in government, 46

Jones, Ernest, 113; dialogue with, 1, 2, 113

Jung, Carl, 5, 6, 85, 103, 116, 117; dialogue with, 1, 2, 7, 112

Kardiner, Abram, 116

Kennan, George, 65

Khrushchev, Nikita, 69

Kris, Ernst, 82

Kroeber, Alfred, 61

Latency stage of development, 25–28

Leaders: as embodiment of character of nation, 69; identity-needs of, related to historical time, 66; as national caretakers, 69; and potentials of nation, 70; rise to power of, 70